GUYANA'S OIL DISCOVERY

MOSES V. RAMBARRAN

GUYANA'S OIL DISCOVERY

PROS & PITFALLS

THE VISION OF A
GUYANESE AMERICAN

PALMETTO
PUBLISHING
Charleston, SC
www.PalmettoPublishing.com

Hardcover ISBN: 979-8-8229-2940-1
Paperback ISBN: 979-8-8229-2941-8
eBook ISBN: 979-8-8229-2942-5

Dedication

I dedicate this book to my parents Kamel Paulette Rambarran and Dennis M. Rambarran, my brothers Paul Rambarran, Dennis Rambarran, Jr. and Michael Rambarran. My grandparents, aunts, uncles and my Fordham family, especially Dr. Richard Langiulli, Frank Scanga, Steven Brown, Louis Adipietro, Michael Savino and Silvio Pietroluongo have all had a profound impact on everything I have been inspired to do and have accomplished. All of you have been a source of perpetual inspiration to me in Guyana and America.

I am also grateful to all my teachers, instructors and professors in Guyana, UK and USA. My maternal uncle Andrew (Terry) Beharry was instrumental in helping us to adapt to the American way of life. He was a source of immense support and inspiration as well.

I am eternally indebted to all of you wonderful personalities. My sincerest and greatest of gratitude!

Mr. Harry Rambarran aka 'Battling Mike'.
The Paternal Grandfather of the author Moses V. Rambarran

GUYANA

Land of Many Waters

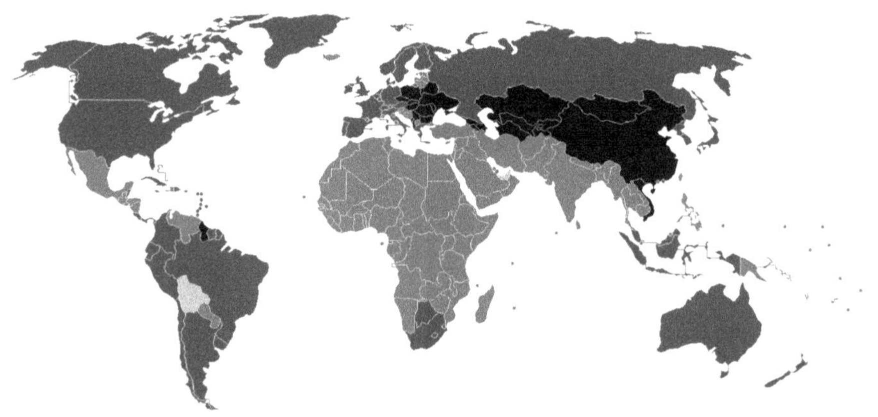

OH BEAUTIFUL GUYANA

Land of Abundant Natural Resources, Oil & Gas, Gold,
Diamond, Bauxite, Manganese, Rain Forest,
Unique Species of Timber, Fish, Flora & Fauna
and more importantly
Beautiful, Brilliant, Hospitable & Industrious People

By
Moses Vishnu Rambarran

Moses Vishnu Rambarran, Esq.

Nurturing family and community are values
inseparable from the Rambarrans.

The strict lady, Mrs. Paulette Rambaran with her four sons,
Paul, Moses, Dennis Jr and Michael

Mr & Mrs Dennis and Paulette Rambarran and their four sons,
Moses, Paul, Dennis Jr and Michael

Table of Contents

About the Author xiii

Chapter

1. Life in Guyana and Migration to the USA 1

2. Education in America 8

3. Guyana's Oil History in Brief 12

4. Standard of Excellence: A Look at
    Norway and Tanzania 18

5. What NOT to Do: A Look at Nigeria 23

6. How the Citizens of Guyana can Benefit from
    Oil and Gas. 27

7. The Resource Curse. 31

    (i)   Implement a Depletion Policy 36

    (ii)   Establish a Sovereign Wealth Fund 36

    (iii) Develop Human Resources Capacity 36

8. Border Dispute with Venezuela 46

9. Challenges in Existing Regulatory and
    Institutional Framework 50

10. Corruption—A Formidable Challenge 57

    (i)   Guyana's Journey to EITI Membership 59

    (ii)   The EITI Standard—A Brief Overview of
           EITI Requirements 63

    (iii) The EITI Board. 79

    (iv)   How can EITI play a more effective role in Guyana?—
           A Look at Ghana 84

11. A Brief Look at Guyana's Existing Fiscal Regime 86

12. Summary of Recommendations. 89

References. 93

The content of this publication reflects solely the views and opinions of the author Moses Vishnu Rambarran. Nothing herein shall be attributed to any other member of the Rambarran family or anyone else.

About the Author

Moses Vishnu Rambarran, Esq. was born in Guyana, where he spent the formative years of his life. He became closely attached to his family, and it remains that way to date.

His older brother Paul used to hold his hand to take him to school in Guyana. Due to a strong sense of determination, inherent in the Rambarran's family, Moses successfully completed grammar and high schools. He went on to graduate from college and law schools. He attended Good Shepherd Grammar School, Cardinal Spellman High School and Fordham University in the Bronx, New York. He earned a Juris Doctor (JD) Degree from Pace University School of Law and was conferred the Degree of Master of Laws with commendation. He later specialized in Oil and Gas Law from the University of Aberdeen.

Moses V Rambarran—
Photo: 1986 Year Book,
Cardinal Spellman
High School, New York

Although Moses considers his outstanding academic achievements and his legal career a success story, nearest and dearest to him are his family and close friends.

Moses Rambarran had nurtured aspirations to run for Guyana's Presidency in 2020. Unfortunately, this lofty ambition had to be shelved when he was diagnosed with multiple systems atrophy (MSA). This severely limits his mobility and speech. Moses was forced to adjust sails accordingly.

Compounding this tragic event, his beloved father and greatest source of inspiration and support, Dennis Rambarran, passed away in 2019.

Dennis Rambarran, with only limited grade school education had actually built a reputable and successful shipping company. He received significant support, through personal sacrifices from his siblings.

The Rambarran Family has proven that great things can be accomplished with hard work, focus, sacrifices and a determination to succeed. This is a message of encouragement which this author would like to communicate to everyone. Especially his fellow compatriots, Guyanese.

Moses was actively involved in sports and other community activities. His hobbies include playing cricket, private pilot training, American football and body building.

Mr. & Mrs. Dennis and Paulette Rambarran and their
four sons, Paul, Moses, Dennis Jr and Michael

Mrs. Kamel Paulette Rambarran with
Jacqueline Jean and Moses V. Rambarran

A Rambarran Family Gathering

Life in Guyana and Migration to the USA

Distinguishable among the early childhood memories is the one associated with the reality of living in a rented house. It was a one-floor walk-up with two small bedrooms and an outhouse. My parents had their room and my brothers and I shared the other. My Mom had to carry water up the stairs to do her necessary chores. At that time, I never felt deprived of anything. However, as an adult, reflecting into my past, it would not be an understatement to say that we were humble people living a very humble life.

The Meadow Bank Residence of the Rambarran Family

Later on, my grandfather, Harry Rambarran aka 'Battling Mike' who had great influence on our family had contemplated gifting us a house. The mere thought of this motivated my dad to purchase a property. My dad acquired a property the name of my mom, for my brothers and I. It was, and still is, located just across the street from the rented house. This new abode had two levels and three bedrooms.

The Rambarran family owned the first wooden shipping vessel in the Caribbean. It carried the name **'Henry R'**. Initially, my dad was the captain of that wooden vessel. As his status improved, he would, on a weekly basis, fly out to Caribbean Islands to check on the ship and its operations. It can be said that my dad did business from his dining room; he never enjoyed the luxury of a real office.

THE 'ALVIN R'

THE 'GRAN RIO'

Dennis Rambarran (deceased) was the eldest of twelve children born to the same parents Mr. Harry (Mike) Rambarran and Mrs. Irene Rambarran. The other siblings in order of age are: Leslie (deceased), Winston, Alvin, Randolph (deceased), Henry R (deceased), Jack (deceased), Jacob, Dr. Moses T Rambarran, Jennifer, and Lynette (deceased).

My dad, Dennis M. Rambarran was a sea captain who morphed into a sensible, street smart, hands-on engineer. He won great admiration and respect from many in the Caribbean. Some time ago, around 2016, on my way to Guyana, it became necessary for me to transit on the Island of St. Kitts. I took the opportunity to go on a tour of the nearby Island of Nevis. I hired a taxi to take me to the closest and safest hotel. On the way, the driver and I were engaged in small talk. I told the driver that I recall when my Dad used to frequently travel to the Ca-

Captain
Dennis Rambarran

ribbean Islands, including Trinidad & Tobago, St. Kitts & Nevis. Sometimes he would have his ships docked at Nevis. The driver astonishingly asked, "is your Dad Mr. Dennis Rambarran?" I was shocked and quickly replied in the affirmative. "Yes he is'.

THE 'FIONA R'

My father was very caring of his siblings. He gave them his emotional and financial support. This expression of care has had a profound impact on me. Despite the circumstances, my father and his siblings always helped each other. I am very proud that I inherited this sincere love for siblings and humanity. This same way, I look out for my brothers and everyone with whom I associate. This character trait of love, integrity, honesty and kindness transcends from the Rambarrans to the benefit of the people of Guyana.

On Sundays, all my uncles would come over to our place and we'd have a cricket match in our backyard. We would have fruits and my dad would be making curry and many other delicious dishes while the kids went to pick leaves by Banks DIH just across the public road, for us to use as a substitute for plates (a local tradition).

My dad gave me the nickname 'Wildy' because I was considered, in comparison with other kids, a pretty unruly kid. My hair always looked like it can benefit from a good brushing. I am also known for running around shirtless.

I had two cousins, Gordon Williams and Morris Mangru, who would jump off the bows of ships with me into the water. My father expected great things from us and always hoped that someday we all will become better than him. He always cautioned about the tough life ahead if we failed to learn from the experiences of others in society. He would often use the common scary Guyanese expression, ***"you guys want to grow up to be cane-cutters?"***. This means that he wants us to study and become educated professionals so that we would not have to make a living by engaging in mere unskilled physical labor.

Home life was very strict. My father and mother made the rules. However, my mother was the enforcer of all rules, which everyone was compelled to obey.

Your hair had to be combed, you had to be dressed properly and you had to practice proper hygiene. Growing up, I didn't realize what a strong woman she was. I only understood her wisdom and strength of her character when I grew older.

Other than my mom and dad, there were a number of other family members who impacted my life greatly. My Uncle Alvin gave me my first job: I had to wake up at 5am, put on my overalls (everyone called me 'Farmer Brown'). I had to catch some live chickens and load them onto a trailer. My job was to take them to La Penitence Market in Georgetown where they had to be 'plucked' i.e. beheaded and submerged in very hot water, have all the feathers plucked out, then the birds are dissected, internal organs extracted and subsequently neatly dismembered for sale. I was about ten years old at the time. I was at that stage of my life where I learned as much as I could from my uncles.

From Uncle Alvin, I learned to have stamina and perseverance; that I must do everything possible to win, be it cricket or doing a school project. Uncle Alvin was the captain of his cricket team. Later in life, I became the captain of my football team in New York. I also admired Uncle Alvin's strength to keep pressing regardless of whatever obstacles may be encountered and in the face of adversities.

The life and work of all my family members have been very inspirational to me. Their names are too many to mention here. Some influential family members include uncle Jacob (Wilfred Rambarran), Dr. Moses T. Rambarran and Winston Rambaran. Uncle Moses T. Rambarran was a unique character. His perseverance is second to none. Despite all odds, and with the love and support of his caring wife Elaine Rambarran, he pursued studies in Medical Science and became a Medical Doctor. He continues to serve humanity to this day. One of their daughters, Serena

Rambarran, is expected to graduate from Medical School in 2023. My Uncle Winston, I vividly remember, thought me a lot. As a little boy, he had me holding a flashlight for him under the cab of a Bedford truck. He knew how the engine worked. Uncle Winston had a trucking service at the time and he had to get this truck ready for 6am next morning. One evening, as it grew darker, Uncle Winston told me to go to bed. As a little guy, I resented and continued holding the flashlight for him. What this experience taught me was that despite all a

Odds, no matter what, never give up. Uncle Winston kept trying everything through the night to fix that truck. I woke up the next morning, looked out my bedroom window into the backyard and discovered that the truck was gone. I was so very delighted and glad.

All my aunts and uncles were loving, caring and encouraging. I don't have a single negative experience with them. They were always ready for the next challenge.

At such a tender age, I was terrified of the idea of going to school. I was very uncomfortable to have to be away from home. I was out of my comfort zone of not having my family's support around me. At school, there were other kids who weren't my family and that probably scared me. However, my older brother, Paul, made me feel comfortable going to school. I think holding his hand comforted me a lot.

The decision my family and I made to migrate to the US can be linked to a particular event that occurred when I was still a youth. At the time, I was attending North Ruimveldt Multilateral School and I was part of the seventh grade. My Spanish teacher called out one of my classmates, asking her "what was so funny?" Her name was Michelle Weathers. The teacher started walking towards Michelle, who sat just behind me.

He was about to execute corporal punishment, as was common in those times. He held his 'wild cane' and was about to deliver some lashes to her. I quickly stood up and put my hands up to prevent him, saying that Michelle didn't do anything. Instead, I received some lashes from his whip on my hands and legs (we had to wear short pants at Multilateral School at that time). In addition, the teacher sent me to the Principal's office and told me to say that I was interrupting the class. When I got there, I told the Principal the truth about what transpired. Lo and behold, for relating the truth, instead of being commended, I received six additional lashes on my buttocks (in Guyana this type of corporal punishment in school was referred to a 'flogging').

Later that night, as I was showering, I remember, how painfully the backs of my legs burned. I had a whole lot of bruises on my legs. My Mother saw the bruises and she completely freaked out. She brought this to the attention of my father. It was at this very moment that the decision was made not to ever send me again to that Multilateral School. It was decided that my brothers and I would be sent to the US to continue our studies.

By the next week, my family (mom and brothers) and I were put on a plane and sent overseas. We arrived in the US in September 1979. My uncle had filed a US immigrant visa petition (papers) for us, but our immigration status was only adjusted in 1987.

The most traumatic experience I endured after leaving Guyana, was the separation from my other family members. I do have a very large family with lots of cousins, uncles and aunts. We used to have fun together playing cricket and football. Secondly, I had to adjust from living in a detached house to living in an apartment in New York. Thirdly, I had a German Shepherd named 'Hitler', that was probably one of my best friends. I later heard that a watchman whacked Hitler on the back of his head. No one told me, but I found out that Hitler eventually died.

Certainly, leaving Guyana was psychologically traumatic for me. The physical separation was perhaps even more difficult for all my loved ones who were left behind, especially uncles, aunts, nieces, nephews and cousins. They were so accustomed to having their four nephews nearly, that our separation became emotionally painful and heart-breaking.

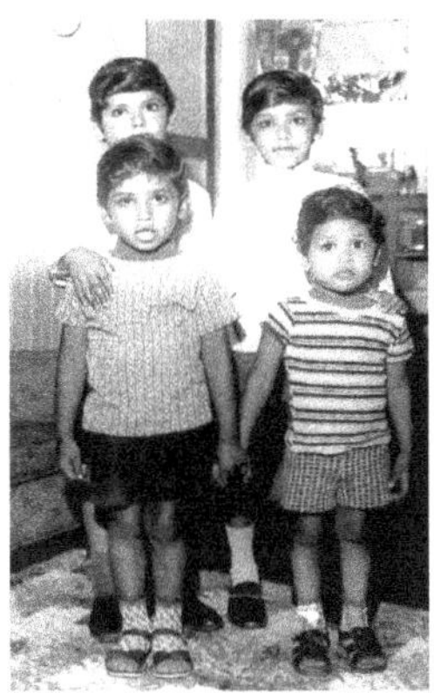

Paul, Moses, Dennis Jr &
Michael at rented house
in Guyana

Moses, Paul, Dennis Jr &
Michael Rambarran at
25 Meadow Bank house
in Guyana

Moses V. Rambarran at
Apartment Building in
New York, NY

CHAPTER 2

Education in America

My brothers and I, when we first arrived in New York, were enrolled at the Good Shepherd Grammar Catholic School. Paul and I started in the seventh grade while Dennis Jr. and Michael were placed in the sixth grade. It wasn't a really big deal to us whether it was a Catholic School or not (we were raised as Catholic), but we had to attend church and observe all the Catholic customs.

Everyone at Good Shepherd, though curious, was very welcoming. This atmosphere was really helpful to us as we were adjusting to a new country with different people, different traditions and different rules. They made us feel special and welcomed. Sports, along with the positive reception accorded really helped me get adjusted to the US environment.

It was at Good Shepherd, while I was in class one day, that I experienced my first snow. My teacher, Ms. Quinlin caught me staring outside in awe. She asked if I'd like to open the window and feel the snow. I quickly and enthusiastically said 'yes'.

After two years at Good Shepherd, it was time for Paul and I to graduate from the 8th grade. This was a big and excited event for our family. My aunt and uncle took a flight all the way from Montreal, Canada to attend our graduation ceremony in New York. Their presence was significant to me. They were always a great source of encouragement to further my education and take my studies seriously.

I attended Cardinal Spellman High School. The four years I spent there were probably the most amazing years of my school life. American football was the main medium of integration. I played together with Michael, my youngest brother. This sport also instilled tremendous discipline in me. It helped me to actually transform away from the rowdy kid I was known to be.

My brother Paul was the model student. I, in contrast, ended up in detention almost every day. Very often my football coach would manage to get me out of detention. I had a reputation and everyone in the school knew me and of me. I used to be able to get away with anything there.

During the summer after I graduated from Cardinal Spellman High school, I broke my collarbone during an impromptu football game. Actually, the ligament which connects the collarbone to the shoulder was torn. I had to get surgery to fix it. This took almost two years to heal. If I hadn't messed up my shoulder, I would have probably been able to play for the Fordham University football team. Unfortunately, I couldn't even think of it.

I attended Fordham University, a nationally-recognized institution. It was considered a great achievement to even gain admission there. It is considered a tough school to get admitted to. I had a meeting with the Dean of Admissions whom I told that I would one day like to become the President of Guyana. He was taken back by my bold ambition. I met some of my best friends while studying at Fordham University. I quickly became enthusiastic and inquisitive about academic stuff.

I was intrigued by psychology as I thought it is somewhat linked to the human mind. I also wanted to get into politics in the footsteps of my uncle Jacob. The University had a prestigious college of business and accounting. I thought about becoming a corporate lawyer. The discipline, teamwork and communication I learned from football probably were key factors of influence on my academic playfield.

I started studying Accounting, but quickly got bored causing me to switch. I eventually graduated with a Bachelor of Science Degree in Finance with a minor in Psychology. Soon after, I was offered a job by a private company. However, late in August 1989, my dad called me and firmly instructed as follows: "I want you to go to law school". I had missed the admission deadline for several law schools. I was left with a choice of three: (i) Pace Law and (ii) St. John's Law in New York and (iii) Rutger's Law in New Jersey. I was anxiously contemplating going to Pepperdine University in California but my parents instantly shot that dream down. I ended up choosing Pace University, School of Law. It was a stone's throw from my home in Westchester County.

I fondly recall that during my first year in law school, my colleagues Ari Bernstein, Paul Zelberfein, Dan Cassidy and I dressed up as members of the group 'Supreme' (Donna Summers) and performed in a part of the 'Rookie Show'. I came to the understanding that what matters most is not how smart you are (I sure wasn't), but instead, how hard you worked.

Fordham University
College of Business
Administration, New York

Pace University
School of Law,
New York

University of Aberdeen
School of Law,
New York

Paul
Rambarran

Moses Vishnu
Rambarran

Dennis
Rambarran, Jr

Michael Rohan
Rambarran

A FAMILY SUCCESS STORY
FROM HUMBLE BEGINNINGS TO
GRADUATES & PROFESSIONALS
SERVING HUMANITY

Wilfred Jacob Rambarran
Graduate
Canadian University

Dr Moses T Rambarran, MD
Graduate
Canadian University

Serena Rambarran, MD
Graduating in June 2023
Canadian University

CHAPTER 3

Guyana's Oil History in Brief

Guyana's participation in oil exploration dates further back than you may think. The earliest records show that flotsam pitch was discovered by Dutch explorers in the 1750's. However, it wasn't until around the second decade of the twentieth century that more significant efforts were undertaken to locate petroleum reserves.

According to records made available from the Guyana Geology and Mines Commission (GGMC), Nelson Cannon, in 1916 drilled three exploration wells in the Waini area in Guyana's North West District. It was revealed that in one of those wells the presence of gas and pitch was observed.

One can say that the unsuccessful search for oil on land continued until the 1930s. According to available research material, a prospective site at Plantation Bath, in 1926 yielded gas adequate for it to be used at the nearby sugar cane factory.

The first oil prospecting license was issued to the 'Trinidad Leaseholds Company Ltd' in 1938. This company partnered with another company called 'Investments Corporation and Central Mining', and embarked on the first collaborative oil exploration venture program in Guyana. After this, still during the British Colonial period, another oil exploration project was embarked upon in 1965. Offshore license were granted to Conoco and offshore and onshore licenses were issued to Shell.

Guyana was officially granted political independence on 26th May, 1966. Bauxite and gold mining together with rice and sugar were major export commodities and foreign exchange earners for the country. However, petroleum exploration remained on the agenda of the post-independence governments.

Our research revealed that there were a number of Amendments made to the country's Petroleum Regulations which the most significant ones can be traced back around the 1967 timeline. An oil exploration license and an oil prospecting license became available to investors. The former was valid for an initial period of two (2) years with the option to be extended for and additional one (1) year. The latter could have been issued for an initial period of five (5) years with the possibility for extension of a similar period. There was an Oil Mining License that was for a period of thirty (30) years and could have been issued for production and development activities.

During the period 1965–1970 a number of unsuccessful onshore exploration projects were undertaken. Nine (9) wells were drilled, but only one (1), the Abary-1 struck oil in the Kanuku license area. During the decade, 1970–1980, the Government of the newly independent country Guyana continued to adopt measures which can encourage and attract investors to engage in petroleum exploration. This was one of the main objectives for which funding from the World Bank was sought. In 1984 the World Bank supported this initiative by providing financial and technical assistance. The World Bank funding was also to help draft and enact petroleum legislations In addition, and of equal importance, a database to serve as a repository for data and information obtained from petroleum exploration was to be established and maintained. The Guyana Geology and Mines Commission has a 'Petroleum Division', which was once headed by Christopher Lynch, a name we hardly hear, but should due to the level of importance of his duties.

In order to get a sharper insight of more developments within Guyana's emerging massive petroleum sector, it is important to study **The Petroleum (Exploration and Production) Act No. 3 of 1986, its various Amendments** and related **Petroleum Regulations**. A comprehensive chart and detailed information database should be prepared and made publicly available. This will certainly encourage and promote more informed debates, especially when country-wide consultations are conducted.

According to existing Laws and Regulations, by way of negotiations, one can obtain a Prospecting License for a maximum period of 10 years. It may cover an initial 4-year period which can be extended twice, but for not more than 3-years at a time. Based on the provisions of the Act, the license holder is allowed up to **6 months to undertake pre-exploration activities. Relinquishment is deemed mandatory**. This can be done for portions or a percentage of the licensed area at given intervals during the term of the license. It might be surprising to note that **mandatory relinquishments exclude the discovery areas**. A **Petroleum Production License**, can be issued if commercial quantities of petroleum is discovered. This **Production license can be issued for a maximum period of 30 years, comprising of an initial period of twenty 20 years and a single renewal period of up to 10 years**.

With funding from the World Bank, marketing and promotional events, including seminars were held in London, UK and Houston, Texas, USA. It might be reasonable to say that this effort probably led to the issuance of two offshore petroleum exploration licenses one to LASMO/BHP and the other to PETREL/GUYANA Exploration Limited (GEL) in 1988. LASMO/BHP concluded additional offshore seismic surveys in

1989. Despite the interest shown by these two companies to explore for oil in Guyana, their efforts did not lead to any substantial action because they failed to secure the necessary funding.

Data and information is vital for petroleum exploration companies. During the period 1992–1994, the Guyana Geology and Mines Commission (GGMC) participated in the South American Mapping Project (SAMMP) sponsored by six major oil and mining companies (**AMOCO, BHP, CONOCO, Exxon, JNOC and UNOCAL**). The objective of this project was to gather aeromagnetic and marine magnetic data on the South American continent and its offshore continental margin. The data obtained was compiled, analyzed and used for the preparation of an information database, including digital datasets. This led to the preparation of a comprehensive report. One would think that access to this information should be restricted and its use closely monitored because of its economic importance to the country.

During the first half of 1994, interest in petroleum exploration in Guyana experienced a decline. The Guyana Government made a decision to persevere/ It entered into an initial six-month promotional agreement in an attempt to re-ignite an interest. The company 'PETREL' was contracted promote and market the offshore petroleum exploration opportunities and attract foreign companies to Guyana.

An attempt at drilling by CGX was made in June 2000 on its Eagle Prospect. The operation had to be halted when the, then, unsettled border dispute between Guyana and Suriname was escalated. The area had to be evacuated because of an invasion by Surinamese gunboats. Suriname alleged that the drilling rig which CGX contracted to do work had violated the national border and trespassed into Surinamese maritime waters.

This escalation caused the Guyanese Government to formally commence binding dispute settlement procedures under the United Nations Convention on the Law of the Sea (UNCLOS). The objective was to resolve the maritime border dispute and bring about a permanent settlement between Guyana and Suriname. During this time CGX acquired 100% of the Pomeroon Block, which covers an area of approximately 2.8 million acres, near to the Guyana-Venezuelan border. At that time, no exploration was in progress there mainly because of the unresolved border dispute between Guyana and Venezuela.

Reports show that in 2005 CGX drilled 3 onshore wells in Berbice by exercising its operating rights in its Joint Venture with 'ON ENERGY'. The 3 wells drilled were Yakusari-1, Hermitage-1 and Albion-1. Unfortunately, all came up as dry holes.

In September 2007, Guyana and Suriname finally resolved their maritime border dispute by way of arbitration using the UN Tribunal of the Law of the Sea. This lured back International Exploration and Production companies, such as CGX Energy Inc, Repsol and Exxon Mobil Corporation to the area. Perceiving that Guyana's natural resources mirror the images of those in West Africa, a number of other companies expressed keen interest in Guyana, including Tullow Oil, Kosmos Energy and Eco Atlantic Oil & Gas.

Later, GroundStar Resources ventured in the Takutu Basin. During this period, oil prospecting in Berbice started to look bright again as the old maritime border dispute between Guyana and Suriname was finally settled. Of the fifty thousand eight hundred square kilometers (50,800 sq. km) that was under dispute, Guyana was awarded thirty three thousand square kilometers (33,000 sq. km) and Suriname got the other lesser part.

The International Petroleum giant, ExxonMobil, in 2008, began oil exploration in Guyana's Stabroek Block. In May 2015, the company, along with its partners China National Offshore Oil Corporation (CNOOC) and Hess, announced that there was a significant commercial oil find in the Liza-1 well in the Stabroek Block. In January 2017, Exxon announced that commercial oil quantities were found in its Payara-1 well. Later on in one more discovery in the Liza Deep field was announced. In March and October of the same year, the company announced two more oil finds at Snoek well and Turbot-1.

In 2018, five more oil finds were announced, this time in the Ranger-1 well, (January), Pacora-1 well (February), LongTail well, (June), HammerHead-1 well (August) and Pluma-1 well (December). Guyana made headlines around the world as the volume of proven oil reserves was considered among the largest in the world in recent times.

Guyana, became the talk of the world in terms of economic potential which is estimated lead to colossal benefits, profits and developments for the next forty (40) years, i.e. until 2060. It is estimated that the country will receive windfall revenues which will be used for massive infrastructural development and improving the lives of the citizens of the country. Economists have announced forecasts of an increase of the population from the current 735,000 to over 2 million persons. Educational and training institutions capable of satisfying the demands of a growing petroleum economy are expected to mushroom. Comprehensive Immigration Laws should also become a key concern of the Government.

CHAPTER 4

Standard of Excellence: A Look at Norway and Tanzania

Tanzania

As we examine the Tanzanian model for Natural Resources development, it appears that the Government did some preparatory work prior to the emergence of the country's petroleum sector. Since the early 1980s Legislations were enacted to ensure proper governance of petroleum. These important Legislations have are being updated regularly as the sector developed. Key Regulations were particularly made in 2015, when vast petroleum reserves were discovered.

Tanzania's Regulatory Framework for natural resources governance is comprised of key laws and policies, including:

(1) The petroleum Act of 2015;

(2) The gas revenue Management Act of 2015 and

(3) The Extractive Industries Transparency and Accountability Act.

The Tanzanian 2015 Petroleum Act instructs the creation of new institutions. Specific decision-making Authorities were established, including the Oil & Gas Advisory Bureau, the Tanzania National Oil Company, the Tanzania Petroleum Development Corporation and the Petroleum Upstream Regulatory Authority. The effective management of petroleum exploration, development and production are coordinated mainly through the work and functions of these Government Agencies. They monitor upstream activities to ensure compliance and also provide guidance and policy advice to the government as needed.

There is an Oil Revenues Fund and a Decommissioning Fund which are supposed to be Governed and Regulated in accordance with the Oil and Gas Revenues Management Act of 2015. The Tanzania Revenue Authority and the Tanzania Petroleum Development Corporation have the responsibility to collect revenues and deposit same to the Bank of Tanzania. The third piece of Legislation is aimed at permanently institutionalizing transparency and accountability in the Tanzanian society. It established the Tanzania Extractive Industries Accountability Committee (TEIAC) as an Independent body, free from political interference. TEITAC has the responsibility to implement the Global Standard of the Extractive Industries Transparency Initiative (EITI). It collects data and information for analytical and reporting purposes. TEIAC organizes public seminars, webinars, meetings and other outreach events, including capacity building activities to ensure greater understanding and public awareness of the governance issues and benefits generated from the exploration, development and use of the country's natural resources.

Norway

The Ekofisk discovery in 1969 on the Norwegian Continental Shelf marked the commencement of a wonderful petroleum journey for Norway. Petroleum production started in 1971. Discovery of massive petroleum reserves were made.

Initially, petroleum exploration was undertaken by foreign companies, which can be credited for developing the first oil fields. In 1972 Statoil,

Norway's National Oil Company was established and the 'principle of 50 percent State participation' was embraced. This principle, like it stipulates, ensures that the Norwegian State has a minimum of 50% ownership in all petroleum licenses. Some degree of flexibility was introduce later when the Norwegian Parliament was authorized to review the level of State participation and determine whether, in the prevailing circumstances, it should be adjusted. In 1985 changes were made in relation to the State's participation in petroleum operations. Petroleum operations became an integral part of the State's Direct Financial Interest (SDFI). Through the SDFI, the Norwegian State gained ownership interest of a number of oil fields, pipelines and onshore facilities. Government's share, which varied from field to field, is determined at the time when the production licenses are awarded. The State, as one of the owners, pays its share of investments and costs.

There is no question that oil and gas has allowed Norway to be transferred into the country it is today. The Petroleum Industry is the largest in Norway. It is the most important source of funding for economic development of the country and the well-being of its citizens in a commendable and satisfactory way.

The Norwegian petroleum industry model, as designed and used, has generated substantial revenues. The country has been consistently experiencing annual economic surplus since oil production commenced. Norway's efficient governance and management of natural resources and revenues are lessons for Guyana, an emerging petroleum giant.

Understanding The Sovereign Wealth Funds of Norway

The Government Pension Fund of Norway is comprised of two entirely separate sovereign wealth funds owned by the Government of Norway:

(i) The **Government Pension Fund Global**, (prior to 2006 was Petroleum Fund of Norway), also known as the 'Oil Fund', established in 1990 to invest the surplus revenues of the Norwegian petroleum sector. In December 2021, it was worth about US$250,000 per Norwegian citizen. It also holds portfolios of real estate and fixed-income investments; and

(ii) The **Government Pension Fund (GPF)**, The Government Pension Fund of Norway is smaller and was established in 1967 as a type of National Insurance Fund. It is managed separately from the Oil Fund and limited to domestic and Scandinavian investments. It is a key stock holder in many large Norwegian companies predominantly via the Oslo Stock Exchange (Wikipedia, December 2022).

It is through the GPF that Norway invests and allocates oil related revenues. It acts as a kind of economic shock absorber when necessary, especially when global oil prices fluctuate.

Ethical Guidelines

Many companies are excluded from the fund on ethical grounds. It is interesting to note that the ***Ethical Guidelines of the Norwegian Pension Fund*** prohibits the investment of its money in companies that directly or indirectly contribute to killing, torture, suppression freedom or other violations of human rights in conflict situations and or wars. Contrary to popular belief, the fund is allowed to invest in a number of arms-producing companies, as only some kinds of weapons, such as nuclear arms, are banned from the ethical guidelines as investment objects.

The Oil Fund is managed by a division of the Norwegian Central Bank. The funds can be invested in equity and fixed income. It is stipulated that 70% of the Fund can be invested in over 9,000 companies. 30% of the Fund is allocated for bonds issued by governments and related institutions, and securities issued by companies, real estate (up to 7% of fund can be invested in unlisted real estate) and real estate renewable energy infrastructure (up to 2% of fund can be invested in unlisted infrastructure for renewable energy).

Avoiding the Dutch Disease

To avoid the Dutch Disease, in 2001, the Ministry of Finance of Norway implemented a fiscal law limiting outflows of cash for government spending. The maximum amount was initially 4% annually. This was an estimation of the yearly return on the Fund's Investments. The aim of limiting outflows was to prevent excessive oil money from entering the economy. This can help protect the value of the Fund itself. Due to this measure, Norway has enabled the value of its Fund to grow over its life time as the **State only disposes of the expected yearly return on the fund**, which was limited to 4% by its 2001 Fiscal Policy. This was reduced to 3% in 2017.

CHAPTER 5

What NOT to Do: A Look at Nigeria

Nigeria

Some people refrain from speaking of a 'Nigerian Model' when it comes to oil governance. It is very common to refer to the 'Norwegian Model'. The Norwegian model is characterized by the separation of Policy, Regulatory and Commercial functions among the Government Ministry, the Regulator and the State Oil Company. Things did not turn out well in Nigeria.

Reform and Chilling Revelation

There have been complications and difficulties in governing the petroleum sector in Nigeria for quite some time, decades. At the beginning of the 21st Century some reform efforts were undertaken. In 2014, the Governor of the Central Bank of Nigeria, Lamido Sanusi, revealed that twenty billion (US$20 billion) dollars in oil sales made by the Nigerian National Petroleum Corporation (NNPC), Nigeria's National Oil Company, had gone missing. In 2013, the corporation's oil was worth an estimated US$41 billion. This was the country's largest revenue stream. The corruption risk was very high, especially when it comes to oil sales. The Nigerian National Petroleum Company (NNPC) never developed its own commercial or operational capacities. It did not engage in external investment.

Very little information was disclosed about NNPC's finances and its operations, despite the fact that its activities have been associated with substantial amounts of public revenues.

Some Government Officials have publicly revealed that they cannot independently verify nor challenge the oil sales figures provided by the NNPC. Many are of the view that the corporation's internal management of oil sales data is very disorganized and poor, to say the least. It is considered too secretive and grossly inaccurate. NNPC officials, hardly face consequences for these irregularities. Investigation have shown that sometimes some persons are sent on retirement and others are transferred to other jobs, instead of been penalized or brought to face any legal consequences for their actions or inactions.

Despite the fact that Nigeria produced substantial quantities of oil for over fifty (50) years, one can say that no commensurate substantial sustainable socioeconomic development are there in the country to boast about. This has given rise to chronic internal instability and periodic violent conflict. Foreign oil workers and wealthy Nigerians have been kidnapped, some of whom were later released uninjured. Oil pipelines and infrastructure have been frequently sabotaged.

In a video produced and released by documentary TV series 'VICE' on its YouTube channel on 22nd March 2018, the consequences of neglecting the Nigerian people have been documented. Rural villagers actually resorted to extracting crude oil from beneath the earth by themselves and refining it in most dangerous ways. The refining process has severely scarred the landscape. Massive fires have ignited frequently at nights at these illegal refineries in attempts to generate the heat required to manufacture the different oil products from crude oil. These oil products (gasoline, kerosene, etc.) are then dangerously bottled and transported via the waterways to be sold.

The Nigerian authorities are very much aware these atrocities. Regular raids of villages and illegal refineries are carried out by the military and the illegally-produced oil products are dumped. This in itself creates an additional unhealthy and unsafe environment. It destroys the flora and fauna and pollute waterways. As a result, the surrounding soil is made unfit for farming. Fishing is virtually impossible due to the mass pollution. VICE also interviewed a few of the Nigerian militants who have said that their intention is not to harm or kill persons but sabotage pipelines to make the oil companies suffer, in retaliation for their unfair, unjust and dishonest treatment of the Nigerian people, leaving them in dire impoverishment.

To combat this situation, the Nigerian government had offered amnesty to the militants. This took the form of a Government Program that was launched in 2009. All militants who unilaterally and voluntarily laid down their arms were told that they will not be prosecuted and that they would be rewarded with several benefits, including a formal education in Nigeria or abroad, small loans to start businesses, a monthly allowance of about US$400. The number of militant attacks reduced sharply. This led to an increase in production. However, a sharp fall in oil prices led to the suspension of allowance payments that were promised to the enrolled ex-militants. The Nigerian Government could no longer fund this remedial project. Tensions were again reignited as large numbers of ex-militants remained unemployed. They grew highly dependent on the monthly allowances that the government was distributing to pacify them.

These are some of the lessons which the Government of Guyana should study and draw conclusions when formulating Policies, Legislations and wealth distribution decisions. The Nigerian experience teaches WHAT NOT TO DO when a country gets windfall revenues from oil sales and the citizens sit in anticipation of receiving reasonable benefits. Oil revenues are expected to bring improvements to each and every citizen instead of sorrow, atrocities, environmental degradation, violence and injustices, while Petroleum Giant Companies take away more than a fair share.

CHAPTER 6

How the Citizens of Guyana can Benefit from Oil and Gas

Oil and gas are valued commodities on the global market. Since its discovery, man has been used it to generate energy for lighting up and heating our homes, to power and maintain transportation such as motor vehicles, cars, boats and planes. With such value, the revenue to be earned by being an oil producer can be massive.

According to the Observatory of Economic Complexity (OEC), in 2020, crude oil was the world's 3rd most traded product, with a total trade of $640B. Saudi Arabia was ranked the top exporter with $95.7B followed by Russia $74.4B, United States $52.3B, Canada $47.2B and Iraq 45.2B. China, The United States, India, South Korea and Japan were the top crude petroleum importers in 2020.

Based on the above-mentioned data, Guyana can be seen as having the potential to earn substantial revenues by exporting crude oil. The question is, **what benefits can Guyanese reap from petroleum revenues?**

The Government of Guyana released an overview of its Gas-to-Energy Project in February 2022. The overview acknowledged that the nation can benefit from the oil revenues. The Government informed the citizens that oil revenues will be used to further enhance economic development in Guyana. It is envisaged that this inflow of revenue from oil sales will stimulate growth in the traditional sectors of the economy, such as Agriculture, Forestry, Fisheries, Manufacturing, Construction and Services.

As per the signed contract with ExxonMobil Guyana Ltd, in collaboration with Hess and CNOOC), Guyana will receive 2% Royalty and a 50% share of Profits after cost recovery. In the Contract, the definition of 'COST' seems to be vague and not consistent with widely acceptable international business practice, accounting and auditing standard. 75% of proceeds from sale of oil can be used to recover 'cost' declared by the Oil Company. The ratio 3:1 is being used to determine how the Oil Companies and Guyana will share the volume of oil produced. Exxon-Mobil, Hess and CNOOC will get the first 3 ship loads of approximately 1 million barrels each and after that then Guyana will receive 1 ship load of approximately 1 million barrels. This means that initially, 75% of oil produced will go to the oil companies (operators in the Stabroek Block) to recover their 'costs', and Guyana will get 25% (Profit Oil). Guyana can make its own arrangements for selling its share of oil. It advertises for oil sales companies to bid to sell Guyana's oil. The selling price is negotiated and agreed between the selling company and representatives of the Government of Guyana. There ought to be a pellucid, publicly accessible formula for calculating profit and how this is to be shared.

Royalty payments and the proceeds from the sale of profit oil are to be deposited in the Natural Resources Fund which was opened at the Federal Reserve Bank of New York, USA according to the Guyana Natural Resources Fund Act. This Act was initially enacted by the previous Government (APNU-AFC) in 2019, but was later Amended by the current Government (PPPC) in 2021 to, apparently, reduce the powers of 'The Minister' and the size of the Board of Directors, among other things. However, many still are of the view that the appointment of the

NRF Board members by the President gives him unrighteous opportunity and advantage to stack the Board with persons, majority of whom will, most obviously, be acting as dictated to by the current President, his Government and the Political Party to which the President belongs, notwithstanding the fact that there will be, among the nine Board members, a semblance of inclusive participation of civil society and the political opposition. There has been continuous active public debates on the effects and purposes of the Amendments. This can be a topic for separate research and discussions in future publications. The table that below provides data which was obtained from the Bank of Guyana website and is self-explanatory.

GUYANA NATURAL RESOURCE FUND—REVENUES DEPOSITED
AT THE NEW YORK FEDERAL RESERVE BANK, March 2020–December, 2022
(PS: data available as at 30 December, 2022)   [USD]

Deposit Date	Revenues from Sale of Profit Oil		Royalties (USD)	Deposits	Total Deposits to Date
	Liza Desstiny	Liza Unity			
11-Mar-20	54,927,994.80			54,927,994.80	54,927,994.80
28-Apr-20			4,919,505.30	4,919,505.30	59,847,500.10
09-Jun-20	35,063,582.06			35,063,582.06	94,911,082.16
03-Aug-20			3,698,152.63	3,698,152.63	98,609,234.79
24-Aug-20	46,046,937.03			46,046,937.03	144,656,171.82
19-Oct-20			4,304,275.30	4,304,275.30	148,960,447.12
11-Jan-21	49,341,810.55			49,341,810.55	198,302,257.67
20-Jan-21			8,332,957.12	8,332,957.12	206,635,214.79
03-Mar-21	50.00			50.00	206,635,264.79
09-Mar-21	61,021,098.64			61,021,098.64	267,656,363.43
20-Apr-21			13,8669,099.18	13,8669,099.18	281,525,462.61
14-May-21	62,617,616.23			62,617,616.23	344,143,078.84
23-Jul-21			12,301,462.65	12,301,462.65	356,444,541.49
28-Jul-21	79,617,561.87			79,617,561.87	436,062,103.36
22-Oct-21	80,373,718.56			80,373,718.56	516,435,821.92
26-Oct-21			17,492,005.29	17,492,005.29	533,927,827.21
24-Dec-21	73,582,168.11			73,582,168.11	607,509,995.32
27-Jan-22			16,087,959.27	16,087,959.27	623,597,954.59
28-Feb-22	95,928,020.91			95,928,020.91	719,525,975.50
28-Apr-22			21,059,488.3	21,059,488.63	740,585,464.13
25-May-22		102,548,225.10		102,548,225.10	843,133,689.23
02-Jun-22	108,556,874.23			108,556,874.23	951,690,563.46
20-Jul-22		122,973,502.40		122,973,502.40	1,074,664,065.86
27-Jul-22	117,445.452.90		51,060,711.00	18,506,163.90	1,243,170,229.76
29-Aug-22		102,543,769.89		102,543,769.89	1,345,713,999.65
13-Sep-22	99,161,132.32			99,161,132.32	1,444,875,131.97
07-Oct-22		88,996,551.12		88,996,551.12	1,533,871,683.09
25-Oct-22			66,947,083.73	66,947,083.73	1,600,818,766.82
07-Nov-22	89,149,227.73			89,149,227.73	1,689,967,994.55
14-Nov-22		87,993,773.93		87,993,773.93	1,777,961,768.48
30-Dec-22			83,808,725.98	83,808,725.98	1,861,770,494.46

Source: Bank of Guyana

CHAPTER 7

The Resource Curse

Many oil resource-rich nations have experienced the avoidable 're-source curse'. A close examination of their policies, economic and social, reveal avoidable mistakes and lessons for Guyana.

ExxonMobil made a historic commercial petroleum discovery. It found vast valuable natural resources, oil and gas, in Guyana in 2017, This catapulted the country to a poised position, among the world's richest, per capita. However, Guyana must take active steps to avoid the 'resource curse' or its people might fail to benefit as much as they should, and the country can become another resource-rich country with impoverished citizens. Many factors are to be studied. This book is an attempt to stimulate interest in the current state of affairs with a view to create greater awareness of the expected benefits and possible pitfalls coming Guyana's way.

A general understanding of the 'resource curse' underlines a failure of governments of resource-rich countries to cause their citizens to not benefit fully from their own natural resource wealth. Research shows that many governments in such countries have not responded effectively to public welfare needs. This led to substantial disappointment and undesirable actions by the population. There are many other reasons for this sad state of affairs.

An obvious example is that of Equatorial Guinea where the statistics show that during the period 1990–2005 infant and under-five mortality rates deteriorated by approximately 20%. Paradoxically, that country discovered oil in 1990 and by 2005 production level reached 350,000 bpd.

Similarly, according to an IMF Study, per capita income decreased in Nigeria during the period 1970–2000. Inequality widened despite the fact that the country earned approximately US$350 Billion from the country's oil boom. In Angola, Equatorial Guinea and Nigeria, oil and gas accounted for 95–99% of exports. This points to the high dependency on petroleum production for economic survival.

We think it is fair and relevant to share these facts for the benefit of the Guyanese people. It can help to understand the existence of ample opportunities for the Government of Guyana to learn from the terrible mistakes of other countries which have fallen prey causing their citizens to suffer tremendously from the 'resource curse'. This 'curse' is often defined as an unfortunate situation, the occurrence of which is linked to a discovery of large natural resources, because the emerging resource-rich nation chooses to focus most of its efforts and attention to the new enticing discovery, mesmerized by the possible massive financial revenues, but reduced emphasis on, even disregarding, its other traditional, existing industries. This phenomenon is often grouped with a resulting increase in value of the country's currency and the Government not adequately addressing the actual needs of the people and the other existing economic activities within the country.

One can say that the Nigerian reality is a perfect example of the 'resource curse'. Its economy became heavily dependent on a few commodities that provide the bulk of export earnings and Government revenues. Prior to 1950s, Nigeria had a mainly agriculture-based economy. However, with the discovery of oil in the late 1950s, the economic base quickly shifted to petroleum production. At this juncture in the economic history of Nigeria, oil production and exports together with imports of foreign goods and services became the dominant economic factors. The country became over-reliant on petroleum development while other sectors of its economy were neglected. This short-sightedness by the Government of the day exposed the country and its people to the whims and fancy of international price fluctuations. The fall in oil prices in 2014 is evident of some of the effects of this mistake. There is an obvious link between this scenario and Nigeria's recession in 2016.

This resource-rich African country's experience has a very important lesson for the Government and people of my native land Guyana. Let it be a wake-up call for Guyana not to ever fall prey to the risk of lengthy reliance on the petroleum, non-renewable, resources. Don't ever let petroleum become, for too long, the country's main or only source of substantial foreign exchange or Government financing.

It is wise and prudent for the country to embark on a serious reform process to diversify its economy, developing its Agricultural, Fishing, Logging, Mineral Mining and Manufacturing capabilities. The economic infrastructure must not be customized only to satisfy the requirements of the petroleum industry, but integrated to simultaneously satisfy the more comprehensive requirement of a truly diversified economic base for perpetual development and prosperity of the people of Guyana.

Angola is another country that experienced the 'resource curse'. It discovered oil and gas in 1960s in its Cabinda enclave. During this period, the country was still a colony of Portugal. Prior to that, its main foreign exchange earners included export of coffee and a few other raw

Agricultural commodities. AT that time, these accounted for approximately 56% of Angola's exports.

Shortly after the discovery of oil, the fight for political independence intensified. However, when attained, the main political factions, which had formed a coalition, quickly devolved into chaos and in-house. Sadly, Angola became an embroiled puppet during the cold war. The ruling faction of the People's Movement of the Liberation of Angola (MPLA) emerged as a dictatorship which concentrated power in a President. The means of maintaining power and self-enrichment were eventually put in place. There was a coup attempt in 1977. The Government of the day began purging itself of rivals. This was brutal. Many people were killed. The country's health and education systems failed miserably, causing untold suffering to the Angolan people.

After the cooling down of the high-powered competing East-West Cold War, (USA, Western Europe versus Soviet Union led by Communist Russia), the internal battle for control of the country continued. It would seem as if Angola's mineral resources provided the political factions, both the prize of victory and the means for achieving it.

The governing People's Movement for the Liberation of Angola (MPLA), which in 1977 adopted Marxism-Leninism as it ideology, assumed control of the country's petroleum resources. It actively sought foreign partners to explore and drill for oil in the 1980s. Angola's oil production increased from 120,000 barrels per day in 1982 to 701,000 barrels per day in 1997. As has been witnessed in many countries where pro-Marxist-Leninist political parties manage to find themselves in power, corruption became a way of life. *On this note, it might be worthwhile to mention that the Peoples' Progressive Party (PPP) which is currently in power in Guyana as PPPC, having included the word 'Civic' to contest the national elections, has always been a Marxist-Lenninst Party. This is fact well documented in national and international literature.* Angola saw signature bonuses deposited in foreign bank accounts and much of the oil revenues were kept for operating secret parallel budgets with little or no public accountability. There was a lack of public disclosure and zero tolerance for transparency.

Though economic growth was recorded after the war due to increased production and record world market prices for oil, little, if any benefits reached the majority of citizens of Angola. Statistical data show that in 2005, GDP per capita increased to approximately US$2,335. However, it must be noted that the distribution of income was extremely skewed. According to John Hammond (2011) Angola's estimated poverty rate was envisaged to be about 68% and the Human Development Index stood at 0.446. The country's overall school enrollment rate was 25.6% and its life expectancy was 41.7 years. The country was condemned as one of the most corrupt in the world. Among 163 countries, Transparency International ranked Angola at 142 with a score of 2.2 out of a maximum of 10.

John Hammond (2011) concluded that secrecy kept the wheels of corruption rolling. As mentioned earlier, much of Angola's oil revenue was deposited in foreign bank accounts. Access was provided to the Angolan Presidency and Sonangol, the national oil company. The Angolan government even threatened international petroleum companies with legal action if they would respond to calls requesting disclosure of data and information. As a case in point, oil giant (British Petroleum) BP, in February 2001, was prohibited by the Angolan Government, from releasing details of payments it made to the Government of Angola. The National Oil company of Angola 'Sonangol' threatened to terminate its contract with BP for violation of 'contractually guaranteed confidentiality'.

The oil company is a major international player with diversified holdings including air and maritime transport subsidiaries, telecommunications, insurance, marketing and trading subsidiaries in the United States, United Kingdom, Hong Kong, Singapore and other countries.

The revenues that Angola earned did not actually benefit the country and all its citizens. 'Sonangol', accumulated wealth and served the President, his family, friends, favorites and cronies.

These activities by Angola's national oil company have led Ricardo Soares de Oliveira, a professor of International Politics of Africa, to characterize the nation as a "'successful failed state'—successful at the purpose for which it was intended, enriching the elites, even as it fails to provide for the country as a whole".

Measures which can help to avoid the 'Resource Curse'

Guyana can Avoid the 'Resource Curse' by enacting legislations to direct the government to:

i)   Formulate, Approve and Implement an Internationally Acceptable Depletion Policy, inclusive of a Phased Production Plan

ii) Establish a Sovereign Wealth Fund with Civil Society oversight and management, unambiguously stipulating that independence from government interference is mandatory.

iii) Formulate, Approve and Implement an Internationally Acceptable Comprehensive Human Resources Capacity Building Policy, inclusive of a Plan with Detailed Programs

Let us now examine each of the above

(i) **Depletion Policy**: Guyana must Avoid the 'Resource Curse'. We believe that Guyana can avoid the 'resource curse' by formulating, approving and implementing an internationally acceptable **Depletion Policy and Plan**. Initially, Guyana must, according to Nick Butler (cited in the Financial Times February 5, 2018), "set the pace of development with a depletion policy". This measure takes into consideration the pace at which oil reserves are explored, discovered, exploited, developed, used for petroleum production and sale. From the point of discovery, the Government has to determine the discovery area and how much of it would be feasible to make available for exploration, development, production and, of course, under what terms and conditions. An internationally competitive bidding process must be identified, adopted and strictly adhered to. Fundamental elements of all of this must include a comprehensive Legislative, Regulatory and Institutional Framework, which will be addressed in future works of this author.

A depletion policy must be an integral part of the fundamental Legislation Framework. The Legislative requirement should include criteria, terms and conditions for awarding license to access acreage concessions to international oil companies. When it comes to National Oil Companies (NOC), an NOC Policy and specific budgetary allocation of funds to the NOC should to be determined by the Government. Funds must then specifically be allocated for the development of infrastructural accessibility to the country's oil reserves with the NOC receiving its necessary share from the State. International Oil Companies usually determine their investment viability by considering a host of economic and financial variables, including machinery, equipment and labor costs, taxation and market prospects. Additional important factors include the degree of political stability in the country and the level of confidence in the government, that it will not renege on agreed Contract terms after investment has been sunk.

Once it has been proven that the oil fields have the potential to allow for the extraction of the natural resources, the Government should participate in determining reasonable production targets. This can be done by executing paramount control and leverage over the natural resources of the country at all times.

This is the stage where corrupt practices have been detected. International Oil Companies and Government officials use various techniques and unorthodox methods to provide biased and unfair share of benefits in favor of the oil companies. Giving bribes to Government officials is common in many resource-rich countries, as discussed above.

Production levels can also be established as part of the depletion policy. In some cases, this can be influenced by a commitment to the Organization of Petroleum Exporting Countries (OPEC), since it plays an important role in regulating the international oil markets.

In all wisdom, Guyana, indeed, stands to benefit tremendously by ensuring that a sound, depletion policy is in place and is executed. International practice has shown that the value of oil in the ground increases more rapidly than the possible financial gains that can possibly be obtained through multipurpose transformation and use of the same petroleum resources.

Phased production over an extended period would reduce the rate of extraction of petroleum resources. This will allow time for local companies to acquire and build capacity so that they can better equip themselves so that they will be able to more meaningfully participate in the operations and management of the country's emerging oil and gas sector. This will provide much needed and deserved opportunities for local businesses and entrepreneurs. A depletion policy must take into consideration, and include, infrastructural development, like ports, transportation hubs, material supply chains, engineering support, amenities and facilities for employees, machinery and equipment maintenance depot and related training and institutional framework, necessary for the smooth and seamless operations of an asset- and technology-intensive industry. We can safely conclude that if the initial pace is too fast, the development of Guyana's natural resources is very likely to become heavily dependent on foreign expertise and services. This can lead to the undesirable effects of delaying or even excluding substantial local content, notwithstanding the recently enacted Local Content Legislation and establishment of a Local Content Secretariat, within the Ministry of Natural Resources in Guyana.

(ii) Many believe **that Guyana should establish a Sovereign Wealth Fund (SWF)** with Civil Society oversight and professional management with fool-proof guaranteed independence from government interference. **The Parliament of Guyana did enact a Natural Resources Fund Act in 2019.**

According to **Sovereign Wealth Fund Institute website, viewed at swfinstitute.org, Sovereign Funds generally do not engage directly in macroeconomic policies. However, exceptions include:**

- Transfers to the budget for exceptional and targeted needs
- Transfer to the central bank for reasonable balance of payments or monetary necessity.
- For Domestic Business Stabilization important for country's economic interest

The legal basis for establishment of a sovereign wealth fund may be:
- Fiscal Law
- Constitution
- Company Law
- A combination of Laws and Regulations

It is known that because hydrocarbons are formed over thousands of years, they are considered non-renewable natural resources. The revenues associated with the exploration, exploitation and use of oil and gas are defined as intergenerational wealth. In this sense, no single-generation should expend them. There are excellent examples where Sovereign Wealth Funds are invested wisely and the dividends are used for economic development and fiscal support.

Guyana can learn a lot about creating and managing its Sovereign Wealth Fund by studying the successful experience of Norway and the United Arab Emirates.

Norway, by way of a 'fiscal rule', has secured its Sovereign Wealth Fund for the benefit of current and future generations. Guyanese should consider similar measures to ensure the country's Natural Resource Fund (NRF) is not used up by any one generation or a few generations. In all fairness to future and unborn generations, only the dividends derived from the investment of sovereign wealth revenues should be used. This mechanism and principle will guarantee that future generations will not be left to suffer after the depletion of the oil and gas reserves, like what happened in some countries. Trinidad and Tobago is an example to study.

A natural resource fund was initially established in 2019 by the APNU-AFC (A Partnership for National Unity—Alliance For Change) Coalition Government by way of the Natural Resources Fund (NRF) Act. The Government changed in August 2020. The PPPC (People's Progressive Party-Civic) Government used its simple majority in Parliament on December 29, 2021 and Amended the NRF Act. It passed the Natural Resource Fund Act, No. 21 of 2021. Guyana can learn from the experience of Norway, which has the largest Sovereign Wealth Fund in the world due to its prudent investments and use of the country's Natural Resource Revenues.

Norway's SWF was formed in 1990, but no saving actually took place until 1996 because of oil price fluctuations which resulted in the Norwegian government receiving smaller revenues than it did in the 1980s

In 2001 Norway formulated and implemented its famous 'fiscal rule' which allows for the conditional use of the oil revenues. If Guyana implements the same, the country can rest assured its oil revenues will last forever, and will benefit both, current and future, generations. The idea of the fiscal rule is to use **"the real return"** of the sovereign wealth fund to enable the government to operate with a permanent non-oil budget deficit, allowing for higher public spending and/or lower taxes than would be possible without the oil revenues.

In other words, relatively large temporary net cash receipts from the oil and gas sector is used to help the government to stabilize its budget. Norway estimated the value of its SWF at the beginning of each year and calculate an estimated 'real return'. This is the amount that can be used to cover the non-oil structural deficit in the Government budget. This deficit represents only the budget balance after the exclusion of oil related revenues and expenditures with cyclical adjustment for taxes and some other aspects of the National Budget. The Norwegian fiscal rule implies that as the value of the SWF increases, so will the spending of oil revenues.

(iii) Formulate, Approve and Implement an Internationally Acceptable Comprehensive **Human Resources Capacity Building Policy, inclusive of a Plan with Detailed Programs and Projects**.

The Guyanese Government should develop and execute a comprehensive National Human Resource Capacity Building Policy, inclusive of plans and detailed programs, not mediocre gestures and packaged political aspirations and vote-catching ambitions. It is no secret that giant Oil companies like ExxonMobil, Hess, CNOOC, Repsol, CGX, Mid-Atlantic, ON Energy, and Total, employ and embrace and respect highly qualified and skilled professionals, unlike the Government of Guyana. These companies easily use this obvious advantage to out-smart the relatively inexperienced Government negotiating team members in resource-rich countries, like Guyana. They might even set out and bribe some of them, most of whom are poorly paid.

Lucrative contracts in favor of oil giants are locked in. In many countries 'under-hand', 'under-the-table' manipulations are obvious. Government officials directly and indirectly are known to have benefitted from oil revenues derived from the execution of legally binding, grossly unfair Contracts that are biased and unfavorable to the citizens of oil producing nations.

The Government of Guyana urgently needs to acknowledge its poor level of expertise in dealing with known oil giants. It needs to take drastic steps to immediately remedy this gap. The Guyanese Diaspora can be a great source of assistance in this regard. Large numbers of highly qualified and trained experts of Guyanese heritage are available. Over the years they have also developed relationships with professionals and associates from other countries with requisite skills and expertise. This untapped, readily available reservoir of much needed human resource capacity should be encouraged, incentivized and lured, instead of being discouraged and despised. Attitudinal changes led by Government officials can make a big difference to attract and employ this unique natural resource to serve Guyana in this time of dire shortage of trained and qualified professionals which the Government itself has repeatedly acknowledged publicly. Proper and sensible Diaspora Incentive Policies should be hastily be formulated and executed.

Government should bring in expertise so that it can become capable to effectively license, regulate and tax its developing oil and gas industry entities. The Guyanese government recognizes the need for capacity building, but needs to be more genuinely proactive to acquire human resources in the oil sector. A proactive, sensible Policy approach will also have a spin-off effect on the country's other economic and productive sectors. Public acknowledgement of real staffing difficulties is necessary instead of covering it up. This will show maturity in governance and opening seen as a source of strength, not weakness, in political decision-making.

Attention needs to be given to the lack of professional quality services and efficient working habits at Government Institutions, Ministries and Agencies in Guyana. Suppressing this fact only makes it worse. Instead, Government should deal with this scourge head-on.

The Government had been repeatedly announcing the rolling out of various Programs for developing and building human resource capacity for first oil. We heard that the Guyana Revenue Authority (GRA), responsible for collecting and accounting for tax revenues, had established an Oil and Gas Unit, the staff of which was being trained with assistance from the US, UK and Trinidad and Tobago governments and the IMF. We heard that one hundred Guyanese citizens have graduated from an oil and gas training school (the TOTALTEC Oilfield Services Academy) to date. They received training in basic safety, rigging and lifting, oil and gas operations safety, environmental best practice, transport and cargo handling, slingers, etc. Staff of the Guyana Geology and Mines Commission's Petroleum Division and the Guyana Environmental Protection Agency also received training on Field Development Planning. This was conducted by Bayphase Oil and Gas Consultants, who, at the time, were advising the Guyana Department of Energy under the previous APNU-AFC Government. Despite all these endeavors, Guyana still has much more to do to develop the human resource capabilities in the country.

Foreign companies operating in the extractive sector in developing countries often bring staff, goods, and services from abroad, with limited spillover to the domestic private sector. Opportunities for direct employment for local citizens are not easily available. Local companies find it difficult to provide services and supply goods to giant oil companies due to inexperience, lack of capital and little or no expertise.

A comprehensive analysis of Guyana's existing human resources capabilities, including a needs assessment and demand determination should be seen as necessary. Information and data obtained from this analysis will serve to inform Policy and help in preparing skills and training programs.

Although the emerging Petroleum sector is very important, all sectors must be given appropriate level of attention and importance as economic diversification must never be placed at the back burner, despite the temptation to do so. Investment in the comprehensive human capital development should become a priority of the Government.

CHAPTER 8

Border Dispute with Venezuela

Guyana has to be wary of Venezuela's claim to its county of Essequibo. With the exploration and discoveries of offshore oil by ExxonMobil, Venezuela intensified its claim to Guyana's territory. This territorial dispute can be traced back the mid-19th century. It includes Guyana's resource-rich Essequibo county. A formal determination of the boundary was made in the early 20th century. Guyana, was then known as British Guiana and was a British colony. Venezuela has been contending that Essequibo is part of its territory and not Guyana's.

The area in dispute lies between the Orinoco and the Essequibo Rivers

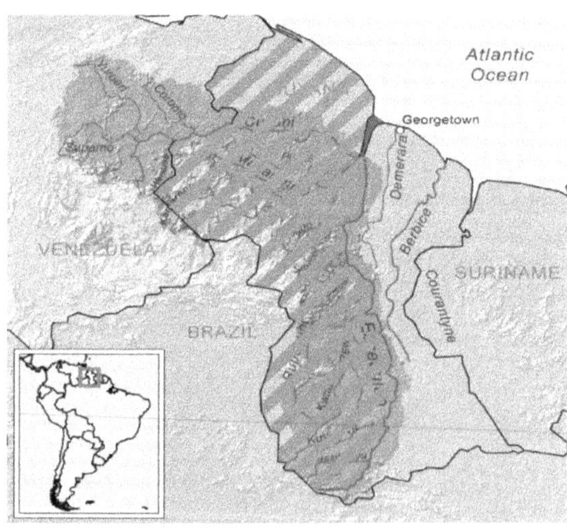

https://upload.wikimedia.org/wikipedia/commons/1/11/Guayana_Esequiba_%28zona_completa%29.png

Venezuela has been laying claim to a substantial part of Guyana's territory on the grounds that it was the successor to the Spanish Empire, from which it declared independence in 1810. However, the British claimed that the Dutch formally ceded to them the area as per the terms of the Anglo-Dutch Treaty of 1814. It should be noted that Spain recognized the Dutch settlements in the disputed area in 1648 when, as part of the Peace of Westphalia, the Spanish and Dutch signed the 'Peace of Münster' that ended the Eight Years War between them. However, this Treaty never really clearly specified the territorial boundary dividing their respective possessions in the region at that time in history.

The German surveyor, Robert Schomburgk in 1840 was commissioned to delineate the boundaries of British Guiana. Some historical documents show that this boundary was disputed by Venezuela. However, in 1850 the parties agreed not to occupy the disputed area. Over time the area saw settlers moving in during the latter part of the 19th century. Later the Venezuelan government expressed dissatisfaction.

The two countries then decided to settle this border and territorial dispute via the International Arbitration process. A tribunal was constituted in France which issued a unanimous award in 1899. Britain was awarded almost 90% of the disputed territory, and Venezuela was allocated a valuable part of the territory, the mouth of the Orinoco river. Both, Venezuela and Per Federica Paddeu and Brendan Plant, 'The Dispute between Guyana and Venezuela over the Essequibo Region' (Cited in *Blog of the European Journal of International Law*, 11th April 2018), both Venezuela and Britain accepted the decision of the International Arbitration process as 'a full, perfect, and final settlement' of the issue" which was in accordance with **Article XIII of the Treaty of Arbitration**. Venezuela did not protest this Arbitration Award.

The Anglo-Saxon Venezuelan Boundary Commission in 1905 established the boundary between British Guiana and Venezuela in 1905.

Venezuela in 1962 declared that it would no longer abide by the 1899 Award and unilaterally considered it null and void. Venezuela, after several decades, hurled accusation that the Arbitration Award was unfair. It started to claim that it was a result of 'a political deal'.

After a series of talks, Venezuela and Britain in 1966 signed the 'Geneva Agreement' to resolve the controversy. Guyana gained political independence from Britain on May 26, 1966 and inherited this opaque border controversy.

Decades after 1966, in accordance with the Geneva Agreement, efforts were made to resolve the border dispute to no avail.

One of the most vital roles of the Secretary-General of the United Nations Organization is linked an option to use the 'Good Offices' as a step to publicly and in private, drawing upon independence, impartiality and integrity, to prevent international disputes from arising, escalating or spreading.

Venezuela and Guyana chose the United Nations (UN) 'Good Offices' option. This allowed the UN Secretary General, in an effort to resolve this dispute, to appoint a 'Good Officer' to do so on his behalf.

In 2006, the UN Secretary General announced that he identified the International Court of Justice (ICJ) as the next means for settling the Guyana-Venezuela border dispute, unless Venezuela and Guyana could find a resolution to the controversy by the end of 2017.

A series of meetings between Guyana and Venezuela failed and the matter was brought to the ICJ in January 2018.

Venezuela argued that the ICJ has no jurisdiction to hear Guyana's case, contrary to a ruling of the ICJ in December 2020.

Guyana sought to have the ICJ validate the 1899 Arbitration Award, which basically deemed as groundless, Venezuela's claims to 70% of Guyana's territory, which mainly is in the resource-rich Essequibo region of the country.

At the time of writing this book for publication, the ICJ is yet to pronounce on the matter. All are anxiously awaiting an arbitration date and decision from the ICJ.

CHAPTER 9

Challenges in Existing Regulatory and Institutional Framework

A Brief Overview

Guyana's rapidly emerging petroleum industry necessitates sound, scientifically based policies and legislations to guarantee the implementation of each and every aspect of those policies. The main objective of any government is to protect the lives of the citizens, collect revenues and allocate revenues to satisfy the social and economic needs of all the people. Let us take a brief look at the existing policies, legislative and fiscal framework, with a view to discussing its usefulness and identifying any scope for possible improvement. We can focus on the mechanism being used by the government to determine levels of extraction of natural resources, collection and distribution of benefits derived therefrom. Indeed, this ought to take into consideration the cost which operators expend in order to extract the resources. In order to successfully achieve this goal, it is important to have a suitable policy as well as the legal framework to implement same. Oil companies should provide details of their financial investments, budget, plan, list of necessary machinery and equipment with cost breakdown.

An essential function and responsibility of government is to formulate and implement policies. This can be a fairly complex process requiring carefully coordinated work of highly qualified professionals working in conjunction with several government Ministries and Agencies. In turn, these entities interact with companies, civil society, and other actors in the various related sectors of the economy.

On December 29, 2021, the Government of Guyana used its parliamentary majority and approved a Local Content Bill and Amended the 2019 Natural Resource Fund Act. The landmark Local Content Bill requires foreign companies to use local businesses and resources for specific projects, including environmental studies and metal fabrication. It paves the way for local companies and citizens to participate in at least 40 critical areas in the oil sector. The government and a number of private sector stakeholders say that this will ensure international oil companies and their contractors utilize more local services and products.

Per the newly enacted Local Content Legislation, a Local Content Secretariat has been established. Oil companies and their subcontractors were given up to December 2022 to prepare a five-year plan, indicating how they intend to employ and procure local Guyanese services.*

[*Guyana: 2022 Article IV Consultation-Press Release; Staff Report; and Statement by the Executive Director for Guyana in: IMF Staff Country Reports Volume 2022 Issue 317 (2022)]

The Natural Resources Fund Bill, No. 21 of 2021 introduced Amendments to the initial 2019 Natural Resources Fund Act. The Amendment provides, among other things, for the following:

- Reducing the powers of the Minister of Finance

- Provide a simpler and clearer formula to calculate the amounts that can be withdrawn from the Guyana Natural Resource Fund for government expenditures.

- Replacing a 22-member Public Accountability and Oversight Committee with a 9-member Board/Committee. The new committee, the Government purports, is designed to ensure practical and effective non-governmental oversight. However, it is obvious that if the President appoints these Board Members, it is more than likely that the deck will be stacked in favour of the Governing Political elite. This is certainly a cause for concern by all, as these are similar methods used in many resource-rich countries where the benefits have been siphoned off to family members, friends and cronies of the Governing elite. In these countries, decisions of the installed 'Board' are subtly dictated by a few top bosses whose priority is to execute their own private 'get-rich-quick' agenda. This pompously eliminates the spirit and real meaning of independence and piles up suspicion and presumption of corrupt intentions. Such a situation becomes even more disadvantageous to the citizens when there is little or no anti-corruption legislation, where law enforcement is deliberately kept weak and monitoring and evaluation institutions are either absent or not allowed to function not in the best interest of the citizens. The poor citizens are left to suffer from all frail, fragile, incompetent and inadequate legislative, regulatory and institutional framework governing the natural resources in general and the mining and petroleum sectors in particular.

- Requiring reports and receipts about of all petroleum revenues be published in the Guyana Official Gazette and establishing a penalty for non-compliance. The Minister of Finance could face up to ten years imprisonment if he fails to publish any petroleum revenue, received by Government, within three months of such receipts.

The Natural Resource Fund (NRF) Bill, signed into law by President Irfan Ali on December 30, 2021, allows the government to extract the entire amount deposited in the NRF, over US$600 million, in the first year after the operationalization of the Fund. This can be used for budgetary spending. After the first withdrawal, the proposed legislation sets out a ceiling on withdrawals, with a progressively smaller sums allowed to be transferred from of the NRF balance to the country's budget.

The Amended NRF Act does not incorporate any verification mechanism of the accountable and efficient management and optimal use of the monies disbursed from the NRF. Public disclosure is not enough. It would be more meaningful to require costs and accounting details of the declared or approved projects, plans, programs and specific activities for which transfer of oil revenues to the budget is intended. The transfer is too general and excludes closer integration with budgetary financing needs, clearly absent is an appropriate and effective fiscal monitoring and evaluation mechanism. While fiscal spending can be increased at a measured pace to address development needs, there is no prohibition clause against any increase in public debt accumulation.

In addition to the GGMC Act, there are several other pieces of Legislations currently in existence which also impact Guyana's Natural Resources governance Regulatory Framework, including:

(a) The Petroleum (Production) Act

(b) The Petroleum (Exploration and Production) Act

(c) The Environmental Protection Act

(d) The Local Content Act

(e) The Natural Resource Fund Act

(f) Anti-Money Laundering Amendment Act

(g) Anti-Money Laundering Regulation

(h) Fiscal Management & Accountability Act

(i) The Mining Act

(j) The Guyana Revenue Authority Act

(k) The Revenue Authority-Amendment Act

It would be almost impossible to guarantee fiscal sustainability without an appropriate and strict Fiscal Policy founded on the basis of Legislations. This should also be seen as an integral element for balancing fiscal sustainability with the developmental needs, being declared by the government in resource-rich Guyana. A prudent oil revenue management framework should also have an embedded robust public investment management aspect. This can be customized to address public demand for anti-corruption guarantees. Limitation on Fiscal Deficit and Public Debt increases should be enshrined in Law and not simply be addressed by political declarations and promises.

Guyana stands to benefit from a comprehensive, unambiguous and integrally correlated Legislative, Regulatory and Institutional Framework with adequately defined non-conflicting roles, responsibilities and functions, all of which can be enhanced with competent legal enforcement institutions.

It would be fair to say that the existing framework and natural resources governance structure in Guyana have great scope for improvement. The President, Vice President, Minister in the Office of the President with responsibility for Finance, Minister of Natural Resources, Petroleum Commission, Local Content Secretariat, Environmental Protection Agency, Guyana Geology and Mines Commission (GGMC), GGMC Mines Division, GGMC Petroleum Division, Guyana Gold Board, Guyana Forestry Commission, Fisheries Department within the Ministry of Agriculture, and other entities must be integrally involved in seamless, coordinated and collaborative roles and functions aimed at achieving the objectives of Natural Resources Governance in Guyana.

EXISTING STRUCTURE OF NATURAL RESOURCES GOVERNANCE—A QUICK GLANCE (Dec 2022)

PRESIDENT—H.E. Dr. Mohamed Irfan Ali
(Former Minister of Housing and Water)

VICE PRESIDENT—Dr. Bharrat Jagdeo
(Former President, Former Minister of Finance)

Minister in the Office of the President with the responsibility for Finance— Dr. Ashni Singh (Former Minister of Finance)

Ministry of Natural Resources

Guyana Geology & Mines Commission

Guyana Petroleum Commission

Guyana Local Content Secretariat

Guyana Geology & Mines Commission—Mines Division

Guyana Forestry Commission

Guyana Geology & Mines Commission—Petroleum Division

Guyana Geology & Mines Commission—Land Management Division

Guyana Geology & Mines Commission—Guyana Gold Board

Guyana Environmental Protection Agency

Ministry of Agriculture—Department of Fisheries

CHAPTER 10

Corruption—
A Formidable Challenge

Corruption—Guyana must decisively deal with this obvious and formidable challenge

There are many examples of massive corruption in resource-rich countries like Guyana. We can learn lessons and how to devise means to avoid such sin. In the oil and gas industry transparency is key for ensuring that if the current and future citizens, who are the rightful owners of the natural resources, receive their fair and just share of benefits. In this regard, the Guyana Government may want to consider giving legal meaning and guarantees to back its public declarations of its intention to embrace transparency and accountability. An Independent Permanent Transparency and Accountability Institution should be immediately established through the enactment of appropriate Legislations and Regulations. It is important for such a body to follow international best practices and be protected against political interference, while ensuring Civil Society is adequately enabled with authority to execute oversight functions.

In addition to the enactment of Legislations, establishing relevant institutions and building necessary human resource capacity must become a fundamental priority of Government. Intensive and extensive training and education programs must be promoted, strategically prepared and implemented. More efficient Judicial, Law Enforcement, investigative and prosecutorial systems should be seen as necessary. A country, like Guyana that does not have these systems in place, ought to, at the minimum, establish and embrace all elements of an efficient, effective and adequate transparency body.

The Government of Guyana announced efforts to inform the world that it wants transparency in natural resources governance. In 2010 a gesture was made to become a member of the global body called the Extractive Industries Transparency Initiative (EITI). The EITI is a global coalition of government agencies, extractive entities and civil society organizations working together to improve openness and accountable management of natural resources revenues. The EITI was established in 2003 as a direct result of initiatives by a number of leaders from some European countries. They believed that if countries, which are endowed with natural resources like oil, gas and minerals, do not properly manage the revenues received from the exploration, exploitation and use of these resources, corruption, conflicts and a lower quality of life may result.

As of December 2022, over 50 resource-rich countries have committed to strengthening the management of their extractive sectors through public transparency and accountability. They chose to implement the EITI, a Global Standard.

EITI member countries are assessed and graded based on actual evidence that efforts and actions have been taken by the country to satisfy each of the specific requirements of the EITI Standard. This process is called 'Validation'. It is actually the EITI's quality assurance mechanism. Countries are required to publish, make available and accessible to the public, comprehensive data and information on extractive sector. These include publishing, on a regular basis, information about the legal, regulatory and institutional framework, data on production, revenue collection, revenue allocation and management.

The EITI Multi-Stakeholder approach, helps to promote better resource governance in resource-rich countries. This has helped to reduce the risk, detect and stem illicit diversion, or misappropriation of funds generated during the development of a country's extractive industries.

10. (i) Guyana's Journey to EITI Membership

Guyana expressed an interest in joining the EITI in 2010. The country subsequently signed a Memorandum of Understanding (MOU) with the EITI in 2012. A Scoping Report, following a feasibility Study on 'The Potential Adoption of The EITI in Guyana', was completed in October 2015 by UK Firm Moore Stephens, LLP.

The commencement of a process to establish a Multi-Stakeholder Group (MSG), in accordance with the requirement of the EITI International Standard, was publicly announced by Minister of Natural Resources, then Honorable Raphael Trotman on 22nd December 2015;

A Secretariat for the Guyana Extractive Industries Transparency Initiative (GYEITI) was formally established within the Ministry of Natural Resources with economist Dr. Rudy R. Jadoopat, appointed as National Coordinator to head the Secretariat. The country benefitted a lot from the rare expertise which Dr. Jadoopat brought to the table. He holds a Doctorate Degree in Economics (PhD), specializing in International Economic Relations and has vast experience in international economic relations and business management acquired during his work in several countries, including Guyana, Russia, UK, Lithuania and USA. The additional advantage of Dr. Jadoopat is that he a son of Guyana who returned as a qualified professional from the Guyanese Diaspora in the USA to serve his native country. Dr. Jadoopat, worked tirelessly and helped to develop Guyana's first internationally acceptable transparency and accountability institution. Guyana's EITI Candidature application was submitted in August 2017. Dr. Jadoopat represented Guyana at the EITI Conference in Manila, Philippines, where the EITI Board, on October 25, 2017, accepted Guyana candidature application which officially made Guyana an EITI Implementing country.

As required by the EITI Standard, a Guyana EITI Multi-Stakeholder Group (MSG) was established and officially launched on February 15, 2017. The Minister of Natural Resources who was appointed by Cabinet Decision as the Guyana EITI Champion, decided that the MSG shall comprise of twelve persons who are to be appointed by the Champion, only after receiving separate lists of nominees, obtained, through open and transparent processes held separately among representatives, from Civil Society, Extractive Entities and Government.

Guyana EITI Multi-Stakeholder Group (GYEITI MSG)
The Guyana EITI (GYEITI) MSG held its first meeting on 15th February 2017, immediately after a high-level official launching ceremony. The Launch was attended by the Prime Minister, Ministers of Government, The Speaker and other Members of Parliament, including members of the Opposition, Members of the Diplomatic Corp, representatives of Civil Society, Extractive Sectors, Oil & Gas, Mining, Forestry and Fisheries. A draft Terms of Reference was adopted. It was agreed that each member of the twelve (12) MSG members would have a designated alternate, to be nominated and appointed in the same transparent manner as primary (seated) members.

The multi-stakeholder approach is central to the principles and operations of the EITI. This is evident in the manner in which the EITI is governed and implemented. Guyana, like all other EITI implementing countries had to establish and must continuously maintain a multi-stakeholder group (MSG) comprising representatives from government, extractive entities / companies, and civil society, the main function of which is to oversee the implementation of the EITI Global Standard.

Building Trust

An MSG is the main EITI decision-making body. It is responsible for formulating work plans with clear objectives in consonance with EITI implementation. It monitors the processes related to, and ensures the, disclosure of data as required by the EITI Standard. A fundamental function of the MSG is to ensure that the data and information contained in the EITI mandated reports contribute to more informed public debates and are used to impact policy and decision-making towards the improvement of natural resources governance.

The GYEITI MSG is a crucial decision-making space for stakeholders and citizens to influence decisions on natural resource governance in Guyana. Consensual decision-making is a core element in the multi-stakeholder process. The EITI Standard requires an inclusive decision-making process throughout implementation with each constituency being treated as a partner.

The Government of Guyana, by virtue of public and international commitment to implementing the EITI Standard, has become obligated to ensure that GYEITI MSG nomination, selection and renewal procedures are in place to guarantee inclusive participation and representation of all interested stakeholders. This is the method that helps to create conditions for a broader and more inclusive management of Guyana's natural resources for the benefit of all citizens and not just a few selected individuals or gangs, headed by pockets of politicians through unfair collaboration with private companies.

The MSG is mandated to determine the rules and procedures regarding its own work and decision-making. The **EITI Standard contains minimum requirements** related to the role, rights and responsibilities of the MSG to ensure efficient MSG oversight of the EITI implementation process.

The GYEITI National Secretariat enables and assists the MSG to execute its functions. The GYEITI initially comprised of a national coordinator, a deputy coordinator/legal officer, a communications officer, a secretary/receptionist and a junior technical officer.

Among other functions, the Secretariat convenes meetings, prepare documents for meetings, coordinate the execution of the MSG approved Work Plan, organize public outreach activities and capacity building events. It coordinates the EITI Report preparation processes to ensure that mandated reports are prepared and published in accordance with requirements and the timeline set out in the EITI Standard. The GYEITI National Secretariat works closely with the Independent Administrator during reporting period.

The MSG oversees the work of the GYEITI National Secretariat, which includes carrying out the day to day administrative and operational functions of GYEITI.

10. (ii) The EITI Standard—A Brief Overview of a number of EITI Requirements

As a member of EITI, Guyana stands committed to satisfy the Requirements of the EITI International Standard. The global body adopted its latest updated Standard in 2019 at its Global Conference held in Paris. Guyana actively participated in this major EITI event. The country was represented by a delegation comprising of members of the GYEITI MSG together with high Government officials headed by the Minister of Natural Resources and the GYEITI National Coordinator.

The author considers it meaningful to engage the readers of this book in a brief discussion on the specific EITI Requirements, given that more than 50 countries have been implementing it.

The EITI STANDARD is comprised of 2 Chapters.

<u>Chapter 1</u> deals with the implementation of the actual Standard. **<u>Chapter 2</u>** speaks about the governance and management of the EITI itself.

At the beginning of chapter 1 you can find the **12 founding EITI Principles**.

- The EITI Requirements expected to be adhered to by Guyana and all other EITI Implementing countries.

- A section of chapter 1 explains how the EITI Board provides oversight of Guyana's EITI implementation process and specify reporting timelines. It also outlines the consequences for not satisfying the EITI Requirements.

- Chapter 1 also outlines a process called 'Validation', an impartial assessment of progress made in satisfying each of the requirements of the EITI Standard.

- The protocol that deals with the "Participation of civil society", and outlined in Chapter 1, Part 6, speaks about requirements and expectations from Civil Society's participation in the EITI implementation processes.

A more detailed look at some specific EITI Requirements
EITI Requirement 1. Oversight by the multi-stakeholder group (MSG)

As mentioned earlier, EITI requires effective multi-stakeholder oversight. A functioning multi-stakeholder group must comprise of representatives from the government, companies, civil society. They are required to independently, actively and effectively participate in the EITI Implementation processes.

The key requirements related to multi-stakeholder oversight include: (1.1) government engagement; (1.2) industry engagement; (1.3) civil society engagement; (1.4) the establishment and functioning of a multi-stakeholder group; and (1.5) an agreed work plan with clear objectives for EITI implementation, and a deliverables schedule that is aligned with the deadlines established by the EITI Board.

The **GYEITI Champion must lead the implementation of the EITI in Guyana. The Government of Guyana is obligated to ensure that an enabling environment exists** for the unimpeded and equal participation of companies and civil society, **without any notion of any hindrance.**

EITI Requirement 2. Legal and institutional framework, including allocation of contracts and licenses

The EITI Standard requires that the Government discloses how the extractive sector is managed. Stakeholders must be provided the opportunity to understand the Laws and procedures relevant to:

(a) The award of exploration and production rights,

(b) The legal, regulatory and contractual frameworks related to the extractive sector, and

(c) The institutional responsibilities of the State in managing the sector.

More specifically, the EITI Requirements related to a transparent legal framework and awarding of extractive industry rights include:

(2.1) Legal framework and fiscal regime;

(2.2) Contract and license allocations;

(2.3) Register of licenses;

(2.4) Contracts;

(2.5) Beneficial ownership; and

(2.6) State participation in the extractive sector.

Let us now take look into some of the above.

2.1 Legal framework and fiscal regime

a) In adherence to the EITI Standard, Guyana is required to disclose the following:

- A description of the legal framework
- The fiscal regime governing the extractive industries, including a summary description of the fiscal regime, the level of fiscal devolution,
- An overview of the relevant laws and regulations
- A description of the different types of contracts and licenses that are issued in order to govern the exploration and exploitation and use of oil, gas and minerals, and

- Information on the roles and responsibilities of the relevant government agencies.

b) Where the Government is undertaking reforms, the multi-stakeholder group is encouraged to ensure that these are documented.

2.2 Contract and license allocations

The Government of Guyana is required to publicly disclose information related to all contracts and license awarded and transferred during the accounting period covered by the most recent EITI Reports, even for companies whose payments fall below the agreed **materiality threshold**. **Such information must include**:

i. A description of the process for transferring or awarding the license;
ii. The technical and financial criteria used;
iii. Information about the recipient(s) of the license that has been transferred or awarded, including consortium members where applicable; and
iv. Any material deviations from the applicable legal and regulatory framework governing license transfers and awards.

In cases where governments can select different methods for awarding a contract or license (e.g. competitive bidding or direct negotiations), the description of the process for awarding or transferring a license could include an explanation of the rules that determine which procedure should be used and why a particular procedure was selected. Where there are gaps in the publicly available information, these should be clearly identified. Any significant legal or practical barriers preventing comprehensive disclosure of the information set out above should be documented and explained, including an account of government's plans to overcome such barriers and the anticipated timeline for achieving this.

2.3 Register of licenses

a) The term license as used in the EITI Requirement 2.3 refers to any license, lease, title, permit, contract or concession by which the government confers on companies or individuals, the rights to explore or exploit oil, gas and/or mineral resources.

b) The Guyana Government is required to maintain **a publicly available register or cadastre system(s) with timely and comprehensive information regarding each of the licenses** pertaining to companies within the agreed scope of EITI implementation, including:

i. License holder(s).

ii. Where collated, coordinates of the license area.

Where coordinates are not collated, **the government is required to ensure that the size and location of the license area are disclosed in the license register and that the coordinates are publicly available from the relevant Government agency without unreasonable fees and restrictions**. The disclosures should include guidance on how to access the coordinates and the cost, if any, for accessing the data. The government should also document plans and timelines for making this information readily freely and electronically available through the license register.

iii. Date of application, date of award and duration of the license.

iv. In the case of production licenses, the commodity being produced. The license register or cadastre should include information about licenses held by all entities, including companies and individuals or groups that are outside the agreed scope of EITI implementation, i.e. where their payments fall below the agreed materiality threshold. Any significant legal or practical barriers preventing such comprehensive disclosure should be documented and explained, including an account of government plans for seeking to overcome such barriers and the anticipated timescale for achieving them.

c) Where such registers or cadastres do not exist or are incomplete, any gaps in the publicly available information should be disclosed and efforts to strengthen these systems must be documented.

2.4 Contracts

2.4 (a) Per the 2019 EITI Standard, Guyana is required to disclose **any contracts and licenses that are granted, entered into or amended from 1 January 2021**. Implementing countries are encouraged to publicly disclose any contracts and licenses that provide the terms attached to the exploitation of oil, gas and minerals.

2.4 (b) The multi-stakeholder group must agree and publish a plan with timeline for disclosing contracts with specific time frame for implementation. Barriers to comprehensive disclosure must be adequately documented.

2.4 (c) Guyana's policy on disclosure of natural resources contracts and licenses must be documented. At a minimum, the government must provide:

i. A description of whether Guyana's legislations and government's policy address disclosure of contracts and licenses. Per the EITI Standard, Citizens ought to know whether the Government of Guyana prohibits disclosure of any contracts and licenses. The multi-stakeholder group should document its discussions about what constitutes government policy on contract disclosures. Any reforms relevant to the disclosure of contracts and licenses planned or underway should be documented.

ii. An overview of which contracts and licenses are already publicly available. The Government should provide a list of all active contracts and licenses, indicating which are publicly available and which are not. For all published contracts and licenses, there should be a reference or link to the location where these are publicly accessible. If a contract or license is not published, the legal or practical barriers causing this should be documented and explained.

iii. Where disclosure practice deviates from legislative or government policy requirements, an explanation for the deviation should be provided.

Definition of Contract

2.4 (d) The term 'Contract' as mentioned in EITI Requirement 2.4(a) is defined as:

i. The full text of any contract, concession, production-sharing agreement or other agreement granted by, or entered into by, the government which provides the terms attached to the exploration, and or exploitation of oil gas and mineral resources.

ii. The full text of any annex, addendum or rider which establishes details relevant to the exploration and / or exploitation rights described in 2.4(d)(i) or the execution thereof.

iii. The full text of any alteration or amendment to the documents described in 2.4(d)(i) and 2.4(d)(ii).

EITI Definition of License

2.4 (e) The term license in EITI Requirement 2.4(a) is defined as:

i. The full text of any license, lease, title or permit by which the government confers, on a company(ies) or individual(s), rights to exploit oil, gas and/or mineral resources.

ii. The full text of any annex, addendum, amendment or rider relevant to exploration or exploitation rights of holders of contracts and licenses.

2.5 Beneficial ownership

a) The Government of Guyana should establish and maintain a publicly available register of the beneficial owners of businesses that apply for, or hold, a participating interest in an exploration or production oil, gas or mining license or contract.

Where this information is already publicly available, the EITI Report should include guidance on how to access this information. Guyana is required to document the government's policy and multi-stakeholder group's discussion on disclosure of beneficial ownership. This should include details of the relevant legal provisions, actual disclosure practices and any reforms that are planned or underway related to beneficial ownership disclosure.

It is required that the Government of Guyana requests, and companies publicly disclose, beneficial ownership information. Any significant gaps or weaknesses in reporting on beneficial ownership information must be disclosed, including naming any entities that failed to submit all or parts of the beneficial ownership information.

Information about the identity of the beneficial owner should include:

- The <u>name</u> of the beneficial owner
- The <u>nationality</u>
- The <u>country of residence</u> and
- If that person can be identified as a <u>politically exposed persons</u>.

It is also recommended that the national identity number, date of birth, residential or service address, and means of contact are disclosed.

The multi-stakeholder group (MSG) should assess and verify the reliability of beneficial ownership information and agree an approach for corporate entities to assure the accuracy of the beneficial ownership information they provide.

Definition of Beneficial Ownership

A beneficial owner in respect of a company means the natural person(s) who directly or indirectly ultimately owns or controls the corporate entity and who benefits from the proceeds of the company or entity.

We wish to let the reader know that the GYEITI MSG, prior to 2022, had discussed, formulated and approved a definition of beneficial ownership. It also approved a definition of 'politically exposed person'. GYEITI MSG also prepared, approved and published a roadmap for meeting the EITI Requirement on Beneficial Ownership disclosures. However, not much has been done to implement the beneficial ownership roadmap or to publish a beneficial ownership register, except for perpetual promises from Government officials.

2.6 State participation

The EITI requires that the Government, if the State participation in the extractive industries gives rise to material revenue payments, discloses an explanation of the role of State-Owned Enterprises (SOEs) in the sector and prevailing rules and practices regarding the financial relationship between the government and SOEs. This should include disclosures of transfers, retained earnings, reinvestment and third-party financing related to SOE joint ventures and subsidiaries. Where the government and SOE(s) have provided loans or loan guarantees to mining, oil and gas companies operating within the country, details on these transactions should be disclosed, including loan tenor and terms (i.e. repayment schedule and interest rate). Multi-stakeholder groups may wish to consider comparing loans terms with commercial lending terms.

SOEs are expected to publicly disclose their audited financial statements, or the main financial items (i.e. balance sheet, profit/loss statement, cash flows) where financial statements are not available.

The Government of Guyana is encouraged to describe the rules and practices related to SOEs' operating and capital expenditures, procurement, subcontracting and corporate governance, e.g. composition and appointment of the Board of Directors, Board's mandate and code of conduct.

EITI Requirement 3. Exploration and Production

Data and information on the exploration and production must be disclosed. This will enable stakeholders to better understand the potential of the sector. The EITI Standard requires the Government of Guyana, in a timely manner, to disclose the following:

(3.1) Details about exploration activities

(3.2) Production data

Production data, including production volumes and values by commodity. This data should be further disaggregated by region, company or project, and include sources and the methods for calculating and verifying production volumes and values, and

(3.3) Export data

Disclose export data, including export volumes and the value by commodity. This data should be disaggregated by region, company or project, and include sources and the methods for calculating and verifying export volumes and values.

EITI Requirement 4. Revenue collection

It is believed that disclosure of data and information about what companies pay and what government receives can inform the public about the governance of the extractive sectors. The EITI requires comprehensive disclosure of company payments and government revenues from the extractive industries.

4.1 Comprehensive disclosure of taxes and revenues

a) Material Payments by oil, gas and mining companies to governments and all material revenues received by governments from oil, gas and mining companies must be disclosed and made publicly accessible, in a comprehensive and comprehensible manner.

b) The multi-stakeholder group is required to agree which payments and revenues are material and therefore must be disclosed.

Definition of Materiality

The EITI Standard considers payments and revenues to be 'material' if their omission or misstatement could significantly affect the comprehensiveness of the disclosures.

c) The following revenue streams should be included:

    i. The host government's production entitlement (such as profit oil)

    ii. National state-owned company production entitlement

    iii. Profits taxes

    iv. Royalties

    v. Dividends

    vi. Bonuses, such as signature, discovery and production bonuses

    vii. License fees, rental fees, entry fees and other considerations for licenses and/or concessions

    viii. Any other significant payments and material benefit to government

d) All government entities which receive material revenues from oil, gas and mining companies must comprehensively disclose these revenues.

In Guyana, all extractive entities and companies making material payments to the Government, GGMC, Guyana Gold Board, Guyana EPA, Guyana Forestry Commission, Fisheries Department of the Ministry of Agriculture and the Ministry of Finance are required to comprehensively disclose these payments.

e) These Government agencies and extractive Companies are expected to publicly disclose their audited financial statements, or the main items, i.e. balance sheet, profit/loss statement, cash flows, where financial statements are not available.

- **Level of disaggregation**

  It is required that EITI data is disaggregated by each individual project, company, government entity and revenue stream.

- **Data timeliness**

  Data and information used in the EITI Reports should not be older than 2 years.

- **Data quality and assurance**

  Data and information about payments and revenues must be subjected to credible, independent audit, and meet international auditing standards.

EITI Requirement 5. Revenue allocations

Information and data about how extractives revenues are allocated must be disclosed by the government so that citizens can understand how revenues are recorded and used in the national budget and in the best interest of the people who are the real owners of the natural resources of Guyana.

Distribution of extractive industry revenues

The Government of Guyana must disclose details about the distribution of revenues derived from the exploration, exploitation and use of oil and gas, mining and forestry resources.

Revenue management and expenditures

The GYEITI multi-stakeholder group is expected to ensure disclosure of information on revenue management and expenditures.

The citizens of Guyana have the right to know what extractive revenues have been earmarked for specific programs or regions. More importantly, there must be a clear and unambiguous explanation detailing the accountability and efficiency methodology used for determining and ensuring the meaningfulness, benefits and 'best-value-for-money' of all and any expenditures.

EITI Requirement 6. Social and economic spending

Citizens can better assess to what extent Guyana's extractive sector has been helping to achieve desirable social goals, especially those which are relevant to environmental impacts and economic outcomes. As mentioned earlier, revenue management and details of expenditures are key and inseparable elements of transparency and accountability.

The contribution of the extractive sector to the economy
The **contribution of the extractive sectors to the Guyana economy** must be disclosed. The citizens must know the size of the extractive sectors in absolute terms and as a percentage of Gross Domestic Product (GDP), as well as an estimate of informal sector activity, including but not necessarily limited to artisanal and small scale mining and logging.

Citizens deserve to know the **amount of government total revenues received and what is generated by Guyana's oil and gas, mining, forestry and fisheries sectors, including taxes, royalties, bonuses, fees, and other payments** in absolute terms and as a percentage of total government revenues.

The Guyanese public must know the particulars of revenues earned from exports of natural resources in absolute terms and as a percentage of total export earnings.

Disaggregated employment figures for the natural resources sectors must be disclosed in absolute terms and as a percentage of the total employment in the country. This information should be disaggregated by gender, company and occupational categories.

EITI Requirement 7. Outcomes and impact
This Requirement appeals to the Author as it coincides with a lifelong desire to make a contribution towards the improvement in the lives of fellow compatriots, Guyanese. He firmly believes that through education and enlightenment, by creating greater public awareness, citizens can impact the management of their natural resources.

The publication of this book is actually premised on the philosophy, mindset and desire of the author, a born-Guyanese, who sincerely wants to make a meaningful contribution to the people of his native resource-rich Guyana. This publication of this book is the first in a series, intended as an initial effort to create greater public awareness about the governance of Guyana's natural resources and how its improvement can lead to greater benefits for all the citizens of Guyana.

EITI Requirement 7 states as follows:
"Regular disclosure of extractive industry data is of little practical use without public awareness, understanding of what the figures mean, and public debate about how resource revenues can be used effectively. The EITI Requirements related to outcomes and impact seek to ensure that stakeholders are engaged in dialogue about natural resource revenue management. EITI disclosures lead to the fulfilment of the EITI Principles by contributing to wider public debate. It is also vital that lessons learnt during implementation are acted upon, that recommendations from EITI implementations are considered and acted on where appropriate and that EITI implementation is on a stable, sustainable footing."

The bluntness of this EITI Requirement can be seen as a **direct appeal to citizens of Guyana** to garner courage and become the master of their own destiny. This is integrally linked to the EITI comprehensive mechanisms for ensuring transparency and accountability in the natural resources sectors. It is seen as an evidence-based management monitoring and evaluation system that has proven to be of great help in a number of resource-rich countries around the world.

Guyana should widely and regularly Encourage, Promote and Conduct Public debates about natural resources governance
One of the main responsibilities of the GYEITI MSG is to ensure that the data and information disclosed by the government agencies and extractive

companies, are comprehensive, comprehensible, accessible by the public, actively promoted and contribute to informed public debates. These public awareness campaigns must get the cooperation of government officials, parliamentarians, civil society, private companies and the media as they are considered key stakeholders by the EITI Standard.

Data accessibility and open data

The government must ensure that EITI reports serve to create greater public awareness and more informed debates about the extractive sectors revenues and management. The EITI Open Data Policy specifically requires that the relevant EITI required data and information be published in digital 'open data' format. This allows for easy download and analysis by citizens. In contract to pdf, 'open data' refers to formats like word, excel, comma separated variables (csv), which can allow for downloaded files to be easily analyzed and reviewed.

Recommendations from EITI implementation

EITI Reports include recommendations and lessons learnt from the implementation of the Standard. This practice helps to strengthen the impact of EITI processes and can lead to improvement in the governance of Guyana's natural resources.

10 (iii) The EITI Board

The **EITI convenes a Global Conference at least once every three years**. At the same time it also convenes Members' Meeting with the three constituency groups comprising of (i) countries (implementing and supporting), (ii) companies (including financial institutions) and (iii) civil society organizations.

It must be noted that the votes of the three constituencies are equally balanced. One of the main tasks of the **Members' Meeting is to appoint the EITI Board**.

Constituencies agree among themselves their membership of the Association and who they wish to nominate to the EITI Board. **Between the Conference and the Members' Meetings, the EITI Board oversees the activities of the EITI** through regular Board meetings, committee meetings and frequent Board circulars.

The EITI Board has 21 members, with the different constituencies being entitled to representation.

The EITI International Secretariat is responsible for the day-to-day running of the EITI Association. A considerable amount of technical assistance is provided to countries implementing the EITI by the EITI International Secretariat and other multilateral, bilateral and non-governmental organizations

EITI Board oversight of EITI implementation

The EITI Board uses a set of criteria in overseeing and 'Validating' EITI implementation in Guyana and other EITI Countries. It establishes specific time frames for publication of EITI Reports and the Validation process.

Independent Validation.

The EITI Board appoints an Independent Validator through an open, competitive tendering process. The Validator will report to the Board via the EITI Validation Committee.

EITI Validation

Validation is an essential feature of the EITI process. It serves to assess performance and promote dialogue and learning at the country level. It also safeguards the integrity of the EITI by holding implementing countries to the same Global Standard. It is intended to provide all stakeholders with an impartial assessment of whether EITI implementation in a country is in line with the provisions of the EITI Standard. The Validation report, in addition, seeks to identify the impact of the EITI in the country being Validated, the implementation of activities encouraged by the EITI Standard, lessons learnt in EITI implementation, as well as concerns of stakeholders and recommendations for future implementation.

There is flexibility which GYEITI MSG can use if it faces exceptional situation that necessitates some kind of deviation from the implementation requirements. It must seek prior EITI Board approval for 'adapted implementation', for which it must explain the rationale.

The EITI Board will only consider allowing 'adapted implementation' in exceptional circumstances. In considering such requests, the EITI Board will place a priority on the need for comparable treatment among of all countries and ensuring that the EITI Principles are upheld, and that the EITI process is sufficiently inclusive, that EITI disclosures are comprehensive, reliable and will contribute to public debate.

Guyana's Standing with the EITI International Body

On attaining the status of an EITI Implementing country in October 2017, Guyana became obligated to publish timely information (Requirement 4.8). It was required to publish its 1st EITI Report within 18 months. According to our research, this was successfully done. Through an open international competitive bidding process, the UK Firm 'Moore Stephen's LLP was contracted by the Government of Guyana to provide 'Independent Administrator Services'. Guyana's 1st ever EITI Report for Fiscal Year 2017 was prepared, approved and published by GYEITI MSG.

At the time this book was being reviewed for publication, Guyana had successfully completed and published 3 EITI Reports for the Fiscal years 2017, 2018 and 2019. **The 4th GYEITI Report, as mandated by the EITI Standard, should have been published by December, 31, 2022**. If the Report is not published by the required deadline, the **country will be in violation and can be suspended if the EITI Board so decides**. If the outstanding Report is not published within six months of the deadline, the suspension will remain in force until the EITI Board is satisfied that the country has published it in accordance with Requirement 4.8. If the suspension is in effect for more than one year, **the EITI Board may delist the Guyana. The GYEITI may apply for an extension of the mandated reporting deadline by providing evidence of 'exceptional circumstances' to the EITI Board**.

Overall assessments on EITI Implementation

The EITI Board makes the overall assessment of progress made in satisfying all requirements in the EITI Standard. It usually would consider the advice and recommendations of Validators and the Validation Committee.

In accordance with the standard Terms of Reference for Validations, the results of the assessment will be documented in an assessment card and a narrative report, containing the evidence, stakeholder views, references and conclusions.

EITI Board Review

The EITI Validation Committee would review the 'Final Validation Report' and the supporting documentation (including the multistakeholder group's comments). The Validation Committee would then proceed to make a recommendation to the EITI Board on the country's progress with meeting the EITI Standard and, where applicable, outline any corrective actions that may be required.

The EITI Board makes the final determination on whether the requirements are met or not. It also pronounces on the country's overall level of progress in accordance with Article 6 of the EITI Board's procedures for oversight of EITI implementation.

Guyana's 1st Ever Validation

The EITI Board expressed concern over Guyana's low score on Outcomes and Impact (42 points).

This low score on Outcomes and Impact, means that there is a lot more to be done to create greater public awareness. This also has prompted this Author to focus his personal time, resources and attention to help Guyana and Guyanese.

According to the EITI Board, Guyana demonstrated an ad hoc approach to outreach and dissemination of data and information on its extractive sectors. It displayed weaknesses in following-up on EITI recommendations to deliver reforms. It paid insufficient attention to the annual review of Outcomes and Impact.

On Transparency, Guyana was given a fairly low score, 53.5 points. In addition, the country achieved a fairly **low component score on Stakeholder engagement (60 points)**. It was noted that while civil society has been a driving force in EITI implementation process, **the Board expresses concern over weaknesses in government and industry engagement in the EITI process, especially with regards to disclosures of required data.**

In 2022 the EITI revealed that Guyana score only 52 points in the EITI Validation

Guyana attained a fairly low overall score (52 points) in implementing the EITI Standard. The overall score reflects an average of the three component scores on Stakeholder engagement, Transparency and Outcomes and impact.

The EITI Board has determined that Guyana will have until its next Validation, scheduled to commence on **1 April 2024**, to prove that the EITI Board proposed corrective actions have been executed.

10 (iv) How can EITI play a more effective role in Guyana?— A Look at Ghana

An oil and gas operation started in the 1970s in Ghana. After some perseverance an offshore oil field was discovered in early XXI Century. Commercial oil production began in December 2010 at the 'Jubilee' field, which was estimated to be only about 60 kilometers offshore. Like in the case of Guyana, when massive petroleum reserves were discovered, enthusiasm and expectations were very high about benefits to develop the country. Some intellectuals were convinced that there would be unprecedented levels of improvement in the development and this would lead to poverty alleviation. These conclusions were expressed after revenue projections were made and correlated with possible socio-economic contributions from Ghana's petroleum resources.

Unlike other African countries like Nigeria, Angola, Sudan, Equatorial Guinea, Congo-Brazzaville, and Gabon, Ghana had no unrest. It was considered democratic State. At that time it had consistent economic growth rates. Before oil, the main export commodities of Ghana were cocoa, gold and forestry products. It should be noted that Ghana was voluntarily disclosing data and information on tax revenues, royalties and rental fees, even before it became an EITI Implementing country. The country gained respect for its liberal governance practices including public disclosures. Its relatively free media and active tradition of civil society engagement in public affairs provided a conducive environment for deepening transparency in natural resources governance.

Civil Society played a major role in promoting transparency through its participation in the Ghana EITI (GHEITI).

Another global transparency advocate, Publish What You Pay (PWYP-Ghana), promoted capacity building events through seminars, workshops, conferences and public engagements based on the country's EITI reports. PWYP-Ghana also conducted a sensitization campaign discussing the challenges and opportunities associated with upholding of transparency principles.

In addition, Ghana established the Civil Society Platform on Oil and Gas (CSPOG) to enhance civil society engagement with the government.

Ghana was recognized by the EITI International Board as an EITI Country that has made meaningful progress in implementing the EITI Standard. In particular, the EITI Validation process attested that capital gains tax and ring-fencing of costs were actually introduced.

The Ghana EITI Validation process had recommended that it should publish a license register. Ghana implemented this recommendation in a timely manner. With this disclosure, the Ghanaian public is enabled to understand the terms and conditions in contracts issued to companies which are licensed to extract the country's natural resources.

Guyana can learn a lot by studying the achievements of the Ghana EITI. The lessons we can gather from the Ghanian experience may help Guyana improve its score in the next EITI Validation and build trust with Civil Society.

CHAPTER 11

A Brief Look at Guyana's Existing Fiscal Regime

The current fiscal regime of Guyana includes, but not limited to the:

(i)   Income Tax Act (Cap. 82:01) revised in 2017,

(ii) Corporation Tax Act (Cap 81:01) revised in 2017,

(iii) Property Tax Act,

(iv) Income Tax Act (In Aid of Industry)

(v)   Anti-money laundering and counter the financing of terrorism Act

As at December 2022 Guyana does not have a Law that exists to specifically govern the taxation of the country's complex oil and gas sector. Despite this absence of Legislation, the PSAs signed between the Guyanese government and the oil companies exempt the latter from payment of the revenues as required for other companies to pay as per existing Tax Laws. These include:

(i)   Value Added Tax,

(ii) Excise and other duties, and

(iii) Property Tax

A common practice for issuance of 'tax breaks', low royalty rates and a greater share in profit oil, to oil companies is to encourage investments during the exploration phases, when risks are evidently highest, as no discovery has been made.

It is only until a commercial discovery is made that these tax incentives are scaled back. In Guyana, there have been enough discoveries made as of December 2022 that implies a need to review contractual relationships and revise fiscal arrangements which were initially made to encourage exploration. Discovery of commercial quantities of petroleum, clearly proves that the prior existing conditions have changed for both parties who signed the initial contracts, oil companies and the Government. They are no longer dealing with massive uncertainty as was the case when the exploration rights were issued.

Oil production commenced in December 2019 and oil export and sales followed continuously since. There is substantial evidence that new objective conditions emerged and do exist. The earlier framework therefore, has legally exhausted its usefulness. This is substantial evidence, necessitating urgent changes to contractual relationships, especially, the fiscal regime that currently governs oil and gas production, export and sale. The Government is now in a far stronger position when negotiating with the Oil giants.

The citizens of Guyana are the rightful owners of the country's natural resources according to the Constitution of The Cooperative Republic of Guyana, the Supreme Law. Owners of anything have legal, social, national, regional, international, and moral rights and responsibilities to ensure accountability, fair play and justice to all. Environmental incidents and accidents in oil producing countries are nothing strange or new. Hence, owners of these resources do have a responsibility to enact and enforce legislations, regulations and policies to protect against the effects of any undesirable accidents or occurrences. In Guyana's case, like in democratic countries, the government is supposed to act on behalf of the owners (citizens) of the country's natural resources. While everyone is in favor of encouraging economic and business activities which can positively impact improvement in living conditions and provide a better way of life, it is of paramount importance that all arrangements, to permit these activities, with consideration given to all related factors, anticipated estimated benefits and possible consequences. The Government must ensure that it will only make decisions which can guarantee that citizens of Guyana will not be 'short-changed' and that they will receive a fair share of the inter-generational wealth. Contracts must include clauses allowing for regular review and updates, because circumstances and conditions never remain stagnant, but instead change frequently. Investor confidence must not be seen as a 'carrot and stick' tool to compromise on fairness, justice and reasonable distribution of benefits. The underlying reason to explore and use the petroleum resources of Guyana is to reduce the level of poverty, perpetually develop the economy of the country and effectuate a reasonable pace of improvement in the lives of the citizens of the country. All and any contracts must be formulated and agreed to, with this in mind or else the scope and quest for fairness in the distribution of revenues, profits and other benefits the will increase and intensify. This can have avoidable catastrophic consequences for everyone, including oil companies, the country, the region and the entire world.

CHAPTER 12

Summary of Recommendations

Among the most important recommendations which this book seeks to highlight:

i. Proactive honest, wise professional leadership by persons with proven track record of integrity and kindness towards everyone, without exception.

ii. Identify goals, assess and determine material, financial and human resources, encourage measured sacrifices with deep focus on achieving objectives and not losing sense of humor, fundamental respect and kindness to family and others.

iii. Value contributions and assistance, no matter how small. Strive to reward everyone for positive input towards achieving targets.

iv. Encourage perseverance and determination during exploratory phases in all commendable and sensible endeavors.

v. Study, develop, enact, establish and enforce internationally acceptable legislative, regulatory and institutional framework, the main objective of which MUST be maximum benefits to all the citizens, who are the actual owners of the Natural Resources of Guyana.

vi. Study, develop, formulate and implement policies and a fiscal regime, specifically to govern and manage the petroleum resources of Guyana, the main objective of which MUST be maximum benefits to the citizens, who are, per The Constitution of Guyana, the actual owners of the Natural Resources of Guyana.

vii. Resolve all territorial disputes in a timely manner and maintain cordial business and diplomatic relations with all countries, especially the neighboring ones.

viii. Study experiences of other resource-rich countries: gather and use the positive advantages to enhance the benefits to the citizens of Guyana. Avoid the pitfalls and factors which contributed to undesirable outcomes and impacts.

ix. Establish a Sovereign Wealth Fund which is focused on creating, maintaining and increasing intergenerational wealth and prohibits the decrease by any single generation. Only the dividends derived from investments of revenues should be permitted by Law.

x. Study, develop, enact and enforce anti-corruption legislation as a matter of highest priority, given the proven bitter experience of many resource-rich countries. The citizens of Guyana must have fool-proof anti-corruption Legislation, with no statute of limitations for corruption related offenses. The must include minimum 25 years imprisonment, cost and seizure of all and any material and financial assets, associated with corrupt practices.

xi. Enact the entire EITI Standard, making it legally mandated to disclose data and information as outlined in it. Enact adequate Legislations and Regulations to penalize anyone and / or all, who are guilty of association with any form of violation of the transparency and accountability standards.

Enact Legislations to guarantee that the entire Government and / or any one or all its officials are prevented from acting or signing contracts and agreements which are not in the best interest of the citizens of Guyana and which do not ensure that the citizens of Guyana will receive greater benefits than any other entity / company involved in the exploration, exploitation, use, sale or export of petroleum and other mineral resources of Guyana.

References

In the preparation of this book, the author studied and researched many published works, including journals, media articles, books, websites and other relevant data and information sources. The origin, significance and helpfulness of each publication cannot be individually recognized herein as the same information has been noticeably, was very often, re-duplicated. Despite this difficulty, we consider it very respectful, and courteous to acknowledge a number of the major sources which stimulated the ideas, views and recommendations that are reflected in herein. The references are in alphabetical order which should in no way whatsoever be construed as any level of priority, as the author has the highest regards and respect for all sources used during the preparation of this work. The author hereby again, extends kindest courtesies to all the individuals who, either individually or collectively, helped to make this work possible.

1. Aaron Sayne, Alexandra Gillies and Christina Katsouris. Inside NNPC Oil Sales: A Case for Reform in Nigeria'. 2015
2. Andrew McKay, 'Black Gold: Norway's Oil Story'.
3. Annegret Machler. 'Nigeria: A Prime Example of the Resource Curse'. 2010
4. Bryan Lee and Kendra Dupuy, Petro-Governance in Tanzania. Opportunity and Challenges. October 2016, 15(14) CMIB 2
5. Centreforpublicimpact.org

6. Durham University. IBRU Centre for Border Research. Venezuela Calls for Talks with Guyana over Border Dispute. 2021, 2022

7. EITI Standard 2019. Oslo.

8. Eiti.org

9. Ejiltalk.org

10. Federica Paddeu and Brendan Plant. 'The Dispute between Guyana and Venezuela over the Essequibo Region'. 2018

11. Guyana Chronicle, December 21, 2019

12. Guyana Extractive Industries Transparency Initiative. GYEITI Report FY 2017

13. Guyana Oil Odessy, 1750–2019

14. GYEITI.org

15. Harvard Halland, Martin Lokanc and Arvind Nair. 'The Extractive Industries Sector Essentials for Economics, Public Finance Professionals and Policy Makers. 2015. The World Bank.

16. James Van Alstine. 'Transparency in Resource Governance'. The Pitfalls and Potential New Oil in Sub-Saharan Africa. 2014

17. John Hammond. 'The Resource Curse and Oil Revenues in Angola and Venezuela'. 2011

18. Kaieteur News. Guyana Daily National Newspaper.

19. Lifeinnorway.net

20. Natural Resource Governance Institute. 'The Resource Curse: The Political and Economic Challenges of Natural Resource Wealth. 2015

21. Nbin.no

22. Nicholas Shaxson. 'Oil, corruption and the resource curse'.2007

23. Nick Butler. 'How Guyana can avoid the curse of oil'. Financial Times. February 5, 2018

24. OEC. 'Crude Petroleum'.

25. Oec.world

26. OilNow.gy

27. Openknowledge.worldbank.org

28. Oxford Analytica. January and May 2018

29. Petroleum. gov.gy

30. Professor John Patterson, 'Petroleum Govenance in Nigeria'

31. Project.iq.harvard.edu

32. Regjeringen.no

33. Resourcegovernance.org

34. Resourcegovernance.org

35. Romina Bandura and Mackenzie Hammond.'The Future of Global Stability'. The World of Work in Developing Countries. Case Study: Nigeria. 2018

36. Stabroek News. Guyana Daily National Newspaper

37. Stabroeknews.com

38. Steinar Holden. 'Avoiding the Resource Curse'. The Case: Norway. 2013. Department of Economics. University of Oslo

39. The Conversation. 'How amnesty efforts in the Niger Delta triggered new violence'. 2017

40. Thecoversation.com

41. Tina Hunter. 'The role of Regulatory Frameworks and Regulations in optimizing the extraction of petroleum resources. A Study of Australia and Norway'. 2014

42. VICE. 'The Battle Raging in Nigeria over Control of Oil. 2015